Michael DeVine

Border Collies

Everything about Purchase, Care, Nutrition,
Breeding, Behavior, and Training

With 56 Photographs

Illustrations by David Wenzel

BARRON'S

About the Author

Mike DeVine has owned and trained border collies for twenty years. He holds a Masters degree in research psychology with an emphasis on cortical functions and learning. He has edited and published *The Southern Stockdog Journal*, an internationally distributed magazine for those interested in working border collies. He is a life member of the North American Sheepdog Society (NASDS) and the American Border Collie Association (ABCA). He currently lives on a farm outside Montgomery, AL with his wife, Lynne, six dogs, and fifty head of sheep.

Photo Credits

Paulette Braun: front, inside front, inside back, and back covers; pages 8 top and bottom, 9 right, 12 top and bottom, 13 bottom left and right, 17 bottom left, 24 top and bottom, 29 bottom, 68, 77, 92, 97 bottom; Kent & Donna Dannen: pages 17 top, 20, 33, 44 bottom, 48 top left, top right, and bottom right, 49 top, 57, 60 bottom, 61 top and bottom, 69; Dee Ross: pages 25, 44 top, 48 bottom left, 72, 89; Michael Ross: pages 9 left, 13 top left and right, 17 bottom right, 21 bottom left, 49 bottom right, 76; Bob Schwartz: pages 4, 29 top, 36, 45 top and bottom, 60 top, 65, 93, 96, 97 top; Judith Strom: pages 21 top and bottom right, 28, 49 bottom left, 52, 100.

All inquiries should be addressed to:
Barron's Educational Series, Inc.
250 Wireless Boulevard
Hauppauge, NY 11788

International Standard Book No. 0-8120-9801-3

Library of Congress Catalog Card No. 97-12565

Library of Congress Cataloging-in-Publication Data
DeVine, Michael, 1946–
    Border collies : everything about purchase, care, nutrition, breeding, behavior, and training / Michael DeVine ; illustrations by David Wenzel.
        p.   cm.
    Includes bibliographical references (p.) and index.
        ISBN 0-8120-9801-3
        1. Border collie. I. Title.
    SF429.B64D49   1997
    636.737'4—dc20   95–12565
                                          CIP

Printed in China

15 14

Important Note

This pet owner's guide tells the reader how to buy and care for a border collie. The author and the publisher consider it important to point out that the advice given in the book is meant primarily for normally developed puppies from a good breeder—that is, dogs of excellent physical health and good character.

Anyone who adopts a fully grown dog should be aware that the animal has already formed its basic impressions of human beings. The new owner should watch the animal carefully, including its behavior toward humans, and should meet the previous owner. If the dog comes from a shelter, it may be possible to get some information on the dog's background and peculiarities there. There are dogs that, as a result of bad experiences with humans, behave in an unnatural manner or may even bite. Only people that have experience with dogs should take in such animals.

Caution is further advised in the association of children with dogs, in meeting with other dogs, and in exercising the dog without a leash.

Even well-behaved and carefully supervised dogs sometimes do damage to someone else's property or cause accidents. It is therefore in the owner's interest to be adequately insured against such eventualities, and we strongly urge all dog owners to purchase a liability policy that covers their dog.

Contents

Most border collie pups develop into alert, intelligent, and willing adults.

Preface

Border collies have become enormously popular in the last decade or so—with the public as well as with advertisers. Such unlikely commercial areas as telephone services and health insurance companies feature border collies in prominent roles. With very few exceptions, no breed has risen from anonymity to popularity as rapidly as the border collie.

However, there is a downside to the popularity experienced by border collies. The demand for them has produced a market that is supplied by reputable breeders but also, increasingly, by puppy factories. Other breeds have had the same problem, with an explosive demand for the breed followed by a decrease in the quality of the dogs.

Border collies have developed over the years into the most useful breed of dog available to ranchers and farmers. Now the influx of inexperienced trainers and handlers offers the potential for a damaged reputation for a breed that at present has an excellent one. Popular or not, the most important consideration in breeding border collies is keeping them intelligent, athletic, and useful.

Acknowledgments

There are many people who have provided information and helped with this book. Special thanks go to Joe Stahlkuppe who provided moral and technical support, as well as talking me into writing it. Thanks to my wife, Lynne, who has encouraged and supported me for the best part of 25 years. Thanks to my sons, Sean and Conan, who tolerated my time spent with the dogs.

More border collie people have helped me than even know it. The late Foy Evans of Hiwassee, Arkansas, helped with insights and a wisdom about the breed that I did not have. The late Dick and Ada Karrasch of Vincent, Alabama, brought with them a beginner's enthusiasm for border collies after working with the breed for decades. R. T. and Blanche Averitt have always been more than hospitable and provided insights from a half-century with the breed. And, there are numerous handlers and trainers, both American and British, who deserve all my thanks.

Special thanks go to Mack, Pepper, Prince, Chip, Sam, Fleet, and Jet—especially Mack. Although more border collies than these have passed through my life, such insights into the breed that I might have received came largely from these fine and loving teachers.

Of course, I must offer particular thanks to the editor of this book, Mary Falcon. Without her hand-holding and help, this book would have been a ragged shadow of itself.

Finally, I would like to dedicate this book to the late W. D. "Bill" Dillard of Matthews, Alabama, who did more to promote border collies in the deep South than anyone has, before or since.

A Brief History of the Border Collie

Background of the Breed

Border collies are a relatively new breed, although shepherds have been using "collies" for centuries. The term "collie" originally meant "black" in some border and Scottish dialects, but over time the term became synonymous with the shepherd's dogs, no matter what their color. The term "collie" is reserved today for a large dog that originated in Scotland. *Lassie* is the most famous collie. Early writings describe the dogs only as being medium-sized, quick, and slender. Photographs taken in the earliest days of photography show working stock dogs all over Britain. These dogs varied greatly in appearance. One picture of a working bitch, taken around 1850, shows an animal with the size and general body structure of the modern border collie but with the wiry hair most commonly associated with Airedales.

Sheep have always been an important part of the economy in rural Britain, and sheepdogs were the core of the economy. Without them, controlling sheep in the open moors and mountains would be an iffy proposition. Sheepmen of the country needed a dog that would move sheep as quietly and gently as possible. They also needed an animal that would do most of the footwork for them. Prior to 1873 there were a variety of working cattle and sheepdogs in Great Britain. The dogs showed all types of hair coat, ranged widely in size, and differed greatly in color. Some animals had white or "glass" eyes, while most had eyes that were one of the shades of brown.

Most of the recent ancestors of the border collie were fetching dogs. Fetching dogs have an instinctive tendency to go around stock and bring them back toward the handler. According to Matt Mundell, a chronicler of British rural life and a lover of border collies, most of the dogs of the late 1800s were a noisy lot. At the large sheep gathers of the time, the normal noise of the sheep was augmented by the whistles and shouts of shepherds and the constant barking of their sheepdogs. Dogs of the day were prone to nip and bite and to move about in the manner of Australian shepherds and Australian cattle dogs. Working style varied from dog to dog as much as physical appearance.

Working Style

Modern border collies are typified by a working style that involves a quiet, head-down style that is remarkably similar to a wolf creeping up on its prey. Instead of barking and nipping excessively, Border Collies use "eye." A border collie with strong "eye" will stare at bunched stock until they decide there are better places to be. Sheep and other stock are as intimidated by being stared at as are dogs. Some people are even a little put off by the breed's tendency to stare at them, but it is not intended to be personal. Border collies are bred to look at what they are interested in; they can be as interested in people as they are in sheep or food or cars—nothing is immune to the border collie's stare.

First Trials

It was in 1873 that the first sheepdog trial was held in Bala, Wales. Prior to this first trial, every good sheepdog in Britain had local support and little other notoriety. Before 1873 the working sheepdog situation was entirely provincial. Every village had a best dog and it was touted to every other village as being the best in the world. The trial of 1873 put sheepdog work on an empirical basis. Every dog ran the same course; every dog had sheep to work that were roughly the same. Suddenly, the top dog from village X and the top dog from village Y could be compared in some meaningful way—good dogs and good handlers had to either put up or shut up. The better dogs were selected for breeding on the basis of their success in trials. It was Britain's system of trials that eventually created the border collie.

The Foundation Sire

Twenty years after the first trial, a dog named Hemp was born in the kennels of a well-known trainer and handler, Adam Tefler. Hemp was a calm working dog that moved sheep quietly and efficiently in contrast to other, noisier breeds. His style of work was so impressive that within a few generations most working collies in Britain had his genes and some semblance of his working style. Hemp is considered the foundation sire of all border collies. Although there have been a number of notable dogs called Hemp, "Old Hemp" refers to Adam Tefler's great dog from the turn of the century.

A Working Standard

Although Hemp provided both the genes and the working style common to modern border collies, the breed had no standard. When the International Sheepdog Trials Society was formed in 1906, one of the first things the founders did was to establish rules for competition; it is this set of rules that has served as *the* standard for border collies ever since. It is a working standard. The dog meeting the standard had to be able do something well: work sheep. It mattered not one bit what the dog looked like as long as it was good at its job. These rules have created the modern border collie.

British shepherds and farmers have always just referred to dogs used to move sheep as "sheepdogs." To this day, border collies, bearded collies, and other breeds are just "sheepdogs" to the working sheepman. It was not until 1915 that James Reid, the secretary of the International Sheepdog Society (ISDS), referred to the breed as border collies. It is likely that name was used casually before Mr. Reid used it but his was the first official use of the name that anyone can find. This, of course, referred to the breed's origins in the border areas of England and Scotland. Mr. Reid apparently felt that the term, "sheepdog" was not specific enough for the dog that his organization was developing.

Modern Greatness

The 1965 International Champion, Wiston Cap, was marked for greatness as a pup. At the age of six months he was already working on the farm, even though it is not normal practice. He won his first trial at ten months of age. At the age of 23 months he won the International Championship. Wiston Cap's performance on the British trial scene was phenomenal. Farmers, shepherds, and smallholders from all over Britain bred their prized bitches to him in just the same way that they had bred to Hemp in his heyday. Not only was he a great worker, but Cap has since proven his greatness as a stud. Three of his sons and two of his grandsons have won the Supreme Championship, a record that does

Except when they are asleep, border collies always seem to be taking in everything around them.

Here we have another indication of the variety in the border collie breed: a prick-eared black-and-white lying next to a quarter prick-eared, merle-colored border collie.

nothing more than underscore the quality of Cap and his ancestors.

The English Shepherd
Border collies and their ancestors have been brought to the United States since the country was founded. Most of the early working stock was brought by Scottish and English shepherds from the border areas of Britain. The British imports combined with British-derived dogs from Australia and New Zealand as well as local American dogs have become the breed known as the "English shepherd."

In 1923 Sam Stoddard of Bradford, Connecticut, imported that year's International Champion, George Brown's Spot. Sam, an expatriate Scottish shepherd, knew the value of the working border collie. Working with Spot, Sam soon let the people of the United States know how valuable border collies could be to the sheepman. They became important after a number of exhibitions were put on at fairs and agricultural gatherings. In later years, Stoddard and Spot would win numerous trials. Sam Stoddard was also instrumental in the formation of the North American Sheepdog Society. He was voted first president and Spot was registered as the Number One dog in the NASDS' books. It should say something about the relative youth of the border collie breed that Spot was registered Number One with NASDS and was only Number 308 with the ISDS, the oldest border collie registry in the world.

Border Collies as Pets
Since there have been border collies in existence, border collies have been pets. Due to their compulsive nature, they are typically herders, obedience dogs, sled dogs, or just jogging companions. No matter what it does as a primary assignment, a border collie is going to be someone's pet.

This handsome male is a classic border collie with a merled coat.

Even if a dog "looks to" one individual, it may go to someone else for affection. In multi-border collie families, one person may do all the training and handling but everyone in the family will have a pet.

Obedience

Border collies have been a powerful presence in the obedience field since they were first admitted to the American Kennel Club's Miscellaneous class. In October of 1995 the border collie breed received full recognition. As of October 1995 members of the breed registered with the American Kennel Club (AKC) have been eligible to compete in all herding, agility, obedience, and conformation competitions sponsored by the registry.

The Border Collie's Appearance and Its Relevance

What do border collies look like? To shorten the answer, they look like border collies. To be more specific, they

The red border collie, the partially merled border collie in the background, and the more common black-and-white male are good examples of the variety of the breed.

are medium-sized and tend to be long-bodied and long-tailed. Like whippets or some of the gazehounds, well-conditioned border collies tend to be tuck-waisted—that is, they tend to have deep chests and very small stomachs. Legs are usually long, though not as long as the legs of grey-hounds or Great Danes. Eye color varies widely within the brown range, with every color from light amber to deep chocolate brown common. Some dogs, typically merles, have white or bluish eyes. Sometimes one eye will be blue, the other brown. Rural shepherds in some parts of Britain have

Border collies come in a variety of colors, coat types, and ear structures.

historically preferred working dogs with one blue eye and one brown eye. There was a common belief that the blue eye saw better at a distance and the brown eye was better at normal distances. There is absolutely *no* scientific support for this belief.

Hair Coat

Hair coat ranges from a coat shorter than a German shepherd's to about the same length as a Shetland sheepdog's. Short-haired dogs are referred to as being "smooth-coated." Animals with longer hair are said to be "rough-coated." Rough-coated border collies may have straight guard hairs or the coat may be crisp or even curly. Some rough-coated border collies will have long, straight guard hairs early in their life that will become crisp or curly as they age. All the coat types are normal. The American Kennel Club physical standard (see page 00) implies that crisp or curly hair in younger border collies may be considered a fault.

The one hair coat characteristic that all border collies have in common is an extremely dense undercoat that holds in the dog's body heat. The longer guard hairs shed rain much like the fringed buckskins worn by American frontier settlers. Smooth-coated dogs are still preferred in the snowier parts of Britain. Longer-haired dogs originate in the warmer, wetter areas of Britain where the long guard hairs serve to keep them dry. Since the short-haired dogs do not have the "feathers" on their lower legs, they do not have the problem with ice buildup that longer-haired dogs do in snowier areas. Even so, the better dog will always be chosen without regard to climate or hair coat. In the border collie world, beauty really is as beauty does.

Color

Are all border collies black and white? Hardly. Border collies come in just about every color a dog can be. The largest number of border collies are black with white and/or tan; black is genetically dominant over other colors. Color patterns are so varied and the number of possible base colors is so wide that predicting color/pattern combinations in this breed is extremely difficult. Even when a dog and a bitch with similar coat colors are mated, the most unusual color patterns may result. First-time breeders frequently become indignant about the "red" dog born to what were supposed to be all black-and-white parents. Some sticky situations have arisen about the "bird dog" in the litter. Usually, the new breeders and the original suppliers come to a peaceful understanding about the border collie's genetic heritage.

• Some border collies are entirely black or nearly so. The biggest portion are, in fact, black-and-white. Black-and-white spotted dogs may be white only on their feet, their chest, or ruff. They may also show white over a majority of their body.

• All-white dogs are rare and shepherds and farmers have traditionally considered them too weak to be effective stockdogs. While there have not been scientific studies in the area, solid white dogs have traditionally been killed at birth. All-white and predominantly white dogs do have a tendency toward blindness.

• Other colors? Sure. Along with black-and-white, border collies come in just about every shade of "red" found in any dog breed. Reddish colors start at flat brown and run to the red of an Irish setter. Reddish dogs may also have white in the same patterns as primarily black border collies.

• Merles—mottled mixtures of dark and white hair—are not uncommon in the "blue" or in the "red" colors. Blue merles have a base color of black; red merles have a base color in one of the shades of red or brown. If you have ever seen a roan horse, you have some idea of the color of a merle. Some black or red dogs may have merled areas where it is more common for black and red dogs to have patterns of white. Merled animals may have merled areas where it is most common to have solid black or red.

• Finally, some border collies may be predominantly black with brown points and no white. Others may be black and white with the same brown points as Doberman pinschers or Rottweilers. These so-called tricolored dogs are common both in smooth-coated and rough-coated individuals.

The Dangers of Breeding for Color

Of what relevance is color to a border collie or his owner? Typically, none.

Occasionally, there are advertisements for kennels raising the "best red working border collies," or "only working merles." Kennels such as these should be avoided. Instead of breeding for the characteristics that have defined the border collie—intelligence and working ability—they have chosen to mediate the selection process by adding another variable. Throwing color into the mix is roughly equivalent to selecting the track

team for a college by specifying that team members must be red-haired *and* fast. It weakens the selection process and, eventually, produces less intelligence and working capability than might have been there otherwise. It is a dangerous trend for the breed.

AKC Recognition of the Breed

After years in the Miscellaneous class, the border collie was granted full recognition by the American Kennel Club in 1995. The Miscellaneous group is the group to which breeds that have not been granted full recognition are assigned. In October 1995 border collies became eligible for conformation and all other competitions sponsored by the American Kennel Club, and, as part of the recognition process, they have been placed in the herding group.

This eligibility was vigorously opposed by several existing border collie registries and special interest groups. One group was founded specifically to prevent the border collie from going on the bench. On registry, the American Border Collie Association recently announced that border collies registered with organizations that promote conformation competitions will have to pass a stringent working test before being admitted to the ABCA registry. The ABCA recognizes all other border collie registries. It is an issue that has not been settled and will not be settled in the foreseeable future. Even though the border collie has been shown in conformation classes in England for several generations, bench trials in the United States have not been well received among working border collie devotees.

In order to be judged in conformation competitions or, for that matter, to be recognized in the Miscellaneous breeds group of the AKC, a physical standard must exist for the breed.

This young, smooth-coated border collie will soon grow into his ears and his owner's expectations.

This red puppy is already showing the longer guard hairs characteristic of rough-coated border collies.

AKC Border Collie Standard

General Appearance

The border collie is a well-balanced, medium-sized dog of athletic appearance, displaying grace and agility in equal measure with substance and stamina. Its hard, muscular body has a smooth outline that conveys the impression of effortless movement and endless endurance—characteristics that have made it the world's premier sheepherding dog. It is energetic, alert, and eager. Intelligence is its hallmark.

Size, Proportion, Substance

The height at the withers varies from 19 inches to 22 inches (48–56 cm) for males, 18 inches to 21 inches (46–53 cm) for females. The body, from the point of the shoulder to the buttocks, is slightly longer than the height at the shoulders. Bone must be strong, not excessive, always in proportion to size. The overall balance between height, length, weight, and bone is crucial and is more important than any absolute measurement. Excess body weight is not to be mistaken for muscle or substance. Any single feature of size appearing out of proportion should be considered a fault.

Head

The expression is intelligent, alert, eager, and full of interest. The eyes are set well apart, of moderate size, and oval in shape. The color encompasses the full range of brown eyes; dogs having primary body colors other than black may have noticeably lighter eye color. Blue eyes are a fault except in merles, where one or both, or part of one or both eyes may be blue. The ears are of medium size, set well apart, carried erect and/or semierect (varying from one-quarter to three-quarters of the ear erect). The tips may fall forward or outward to the side. The ears are sensitive and mobile. The skull is broad

The piebald pattern of this prick-eared border collie is not only attractive, it is relatively common.

While she may appear to be thinking, this border collie is just waiting for her next command.

Characteristics that trainers find attractive—intelligence and attentiveness—are evident in this border collie.

Looking at this handsome youngster, it is not hard to understand why some people prefer red border collies.

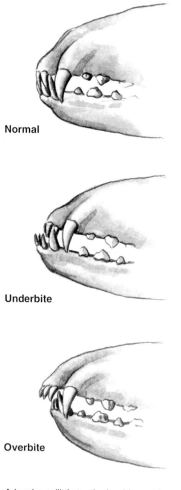

Normal

Underbite

Overbite

A border collie's teeth should meet in a scissor bite. Underbites and overbites are faults.

with occiput not pronounced. The skull and foreface are approximately equal in length. The stop is moderate, but distinct. The muzzle is moderately short, strong, and blunt, tapering to the nose. The underjaw is strong and well developed. The nose color generally matches the primary body color.

Nostrils are well developed. A snipy muzzle is a fault. Bite: The teeth and jaws are strong, meeting in a scissor bite.

Neck, Topline, and Body

The neck is of good length, strong and muscular, slightly arched, and broadening to the shoulders. The topline is level, with a slight arch over the loins. The body is athletic in appearance. The chest is deep, moderately broad, showing great lung capacity. The brisket reaches to the point of the elbow. The rib cage is well sprung. The loins are moderately deep, muscular, and slightly arched, with no tuck-up. The croup slopes gradually downward. The tail is set low. It is moderately long, bone reaching at least to the hock. It may have an upward swirl to the tip. While the dog is concentrating at a given task, the tail is carried low and used for balance. In excitement it may rise level with the back. A "gay" tail is a fault.

Forequarters

The forelegs are well-boned and parallel when viewed from the front, the pasterns slightly sloping when viewed from the side. The shoulders are long and well-angulated to the upper arm. The elbows are neither in nor out. The dewclaws may be removed. The feet are compact, oval in shape, the pads deep and strong, the toes moderately arched and close together.

Hindquarters

Broad and muscular, in profile sloping gracefully to the set of the tail. The thighs are long, broad, deep, and muscular, with well-turned stifles and strong hocks well let down. When viewed from the rear, hind legs are well-boned, straight, and parallel, or are very slightly cowhocked. The dewclaws may be removed. The feet are compact, oval in shape, the pads deep and strong, the toes moderately arched and close together. The nails are short and strong.

Coat

Two varieties are permissible, both having a soft, dense, weather-resistant double coat. In puppies, the coat is short, soft, dense, and water resistant, becoming the undercoat in adult dogs. The rough coat is of medium to long texture, from flat to slightly wavy. There is a short and smooth coat on the face. The forelegs are feathered. The rear pasterns may have the coat trimmed short. With advancing age, coats may become very wavy and are not faulted. The smooth coat is short over the entire body. There may be feathering on the forelegs and a fuller coat on the chest.

Color

The border collie appears in many colors, with various combinations of patterns and markings. The most common color is black with or without the traditional white blaze, collar, stockings, and tail tip, with or without tan points. However, a variety of primary body colors is permissible, the sole exception being all white. Solid color, bicolor, tricolor, merle, and sable dogs are judged equally with dogs having traditional markings. Color and marking are always secondary to physical evaluation and gait.

Gait

The border collie is an agile dog, able to suddenly change speed and direction without loss of balance and grace. Endurance is its trademark. Its trotting gait is free, smooth, and tireless, with a minimum lift of feet. The topline does not shift as it conveys an effortless glide. It moves with great stealth, strength, and stamina. When viewed from the side, the stride should cover maximum ground, with minimum speed. Viewed from the front, the action is forward and true, without weakness in the shoulders, elbows, or pasterns. Viewed from behind, the quarters thrust with drive and flexibility, with the hocks moving close together but never touching. Any deviation from a sound-moving dog is a fault. In the final assessment, gait is an essential factor, confirming physical evaluation.

Temperament

The border collie is intelligent, alert, and responsive. Affectionate toward friends, it may be sensibly reserved toward strangers, and therefore makes an excellent watchdog. An intensive worker while herding, it is eager to learn and to please, and thrives on human companionship. Any tendencies toward viciousness or extreme shyness are serious faults.

Are You Border Collie Material?

The answer to the question posed in the title of this section is, "Probably not." The characteristics required of a border collie owner are complex and uncommon. This chapter will deal with what it takes to be a border collie owner.

Lifestyles

City Dwellers

Border collies can live well in the city if they are given plenty of exercise, something to do, a great deal of attention, and a lot of time. If you live in the city and are exploring the possibility of getting a border collie, ask yourself the following questions:

Once they are housebroken, border collies make great family dogs.

1. How much are you home?
2. Does your job require you to travel with any frequency?
3. What do you enjoy doing in your off hours?
4. Are there facilities close to your home for exercising your pet?
5. Do you have the interest and the time to engage in obedience, agility, or other forms of training?

You do not have to sacrifice your social life, abandon your spouse, or give up other interests to own a border collie, but you will have to make adjustments. If you live alone and travel as a regular part of your job, consider another breed. If you do not live within easy commuting range of obedience classes, jogging tracks, and/or a park, perhaps some other dog will serve you better. Finally, if you had rather spend time at a sports bar, a concert, or an athletic event than working your border collie, do yourself a favor and buy a stuffed dog.

If you cannot be home at a predictable hour, border collies are not for you. For that matter, if you cannot make it home at a predictable hour, no breed is really for you, but if you are a city dweller thinking about a border collie, examine your life closely before you commit.

Border Collies in the Suburbs

Suburbanites have to ask themselves the same questions about their time and their willingness to share it with a border collie. Living in the suburbs may have the disadvantage of a

Children and border collies are a natural combination if the child is trained to respect the dog.

The head-down stalking style is one of the characteristics of the border collie's working style.

The red border collie has every characteristic of the border collie breed, plus genes for a red coat.

Some border collies are natural escape artists. Be sure that your kennel or yard is escape-proof.

if especially bored. Make sure your neighbors will not be offended by the occasional bout of barking.

You will have to do everything in your power to make sure that your border collie will not be nuisance to the neighborhood. It should be in its own yard at all times when it is not on a leash. A well-bred, handsome border collie tunneling through a flower bed is no more acceptable to your neighbor than having a mangy mixed-breed do the same thing. In fact, the mangy mixed-breed has a certain advantage over your border collie, since your neighbor will know where your dog lives.

To make your dog happier in the suburbs, consider providing your border collie with the following:

1. A yard that is fenced with wiring and that is escape-proof.

2. A play area for your border collie that will allow it to dig to its heart's content. Sandboxes are ideal for this.

3. A yard cleared of the toxic plants and other safety hazards that could cause your pet harm.

4. A supply of toys for your border collie in its play area. This will not only give it something to do, it will help keep it out of trouble in other areas of the yard.

5. Constant anti-chasing training. Discourage your dog from chasing the neighborhood cats. It will not only keep it from getting in bad with your neighbors, but could well save it injury or death if it ever escapes your yard.

Country Border Collies

Even if you live in the country you may not be border collie material. The questions asked of the city dweller apply to people from the country, too. Do you have the time to devote to a border collie? If you live in the country and commute to the city to work, you may not be in any better shape than the suburbanite or city dweller.

longer commute to work, providing less time for you to spend with your border collie, but there may be offsetting advantages in the easy availability of veterinary services, places to exercise your border collie, and the accessibility of obedience classes and trials. Similarly, suburban life will offer the choice of keeping your border collie in the house, in the yard, or some combination of the two.

If you do live in the suburbs, consider the neighbors. Most suburban areas are relatively lax in their control of dogs. Border collies are not especially prone to barking but they *are* dogs and they may bark excessively

Obviously, cattle and sheep ranchers have a use for border collies. Exercise is typically not an issue on a ranch, but housing will be an issue, even in the country. The country border collie will need the same dry, draft-proof housing as its suburban or city cousins. For the country dog, the outside kennel is more practical than other forms of housing. True, border collies can live in country homes as well as they can live in urban apartments. Problems may arise in the country because the country border collie, particularly working dogs, regularly come in contact with substances most homeowners do not want in their houses. The outside kennel offers warmth, protection from the elements, and a high level of sanitation.

Another issue that may be even more important for the country border collie than for those in the city or the suburbs is grooming. Working dogs and those nonworking border collies that frequent the fields and forests are exposed to the burrs and briars that grow there. These briars and burrs cause matting if they are not removed as quickly as possible. The regular grooming recommended for the city is even more important for the country border collie; rough-coated border collies are especially at risk (see Border Collie Care, beginning on page 32).

How to Find a Border Collie

As border collies' popularity has grown in recent years, they have become progressively easier to find. Finding a border collie 20 years ago required focused detective work unless you were already in touch with border collie people. Today, it is almost impossible to open a newspaper, an agricultural bulletin, or shopper's guide without encountering at least one ad for a border collie for sale. The question is, where should you go to find a border collie? There is a simple answer to this

Digging is one of the potential problems you may encounter if you keep your border collie in a fenced yard. Their energy should be channeled to more positive activities.

question: Find a farmer, or a rancher, or someone else who has a litter of border collie pups from working stock and buy one. An adult border collie from working stock will serve just as well if it has not been spoiled in some way.

Obedience handlers frequently own more than one breed of dog. They buy most of their dogs, border collie or otherwise, and rarely breed them. It is the farmer, the rancher, or the trialing enthusiast who will be more prone to breed border collies. Even the larger cities have access to farms or ranches. Time spent driving to a ranch or farm to look over puppies is time well invested. If ranchers and/or farmers in the region do not have puppies, most of the registries and clubs listed in the back of this book can give you the information you need. They will not, of course, recommend one breeder over another, but they will provide a list of members. Some maintain lists of members who breed their border collies. These lists are provided free or at low cost.

Tweed watches his master closely to make sure there are no errors.

Selecting the Right Border Collie

Aside from the few physical and psychological characteristics that make border collies unique, the individuals in the breed vary widely. Some border collies are aggressive and confident; others are shy and withdrawn.

Adult or Puppy?

What are the advantages of an adult border collie over a puppy? Adult border collies have gone through the growing pains, puppy illnesses, housebreaking, and teething. They are what they will be, allowing for a little training.

If you choose to go with an adult border collie, be certain that you understand its personality and that it is compatible with your needs. A shy dog will not fit the needs of a cattle rancher but may be an ideal house pet and companion.

However, depending upon how they have been treated in their lives, adult border collies may bring a great deal of baggage with them when they arrive. Most adult border collies have been raised by caring, careful owners who must find a new home for their pets when changes occur in their lives, but unfortunately, some border collies have not been well treated. Abused or ignored dogs will have difficulty trusting a new family. Worse, border collies that have been penned and ignored may never develop the intelligence that is their birthright.

If you decide on a puppy, remember that puppies are nothing more than fur-covered potential. What they can become is already defined in their genetic structure. Of course, genes are contributed by their ancestors through their parents; therefore, their parents are important to what they may become. The environment and treatment the pup receives are critical to the development of its unique personality.

Puppies have the advantage of being yours to mold. Border collies will learn your idiosyncrasies as they mature. Their personality will develop as a function of *your* personality. Given the right puppy and intelligent, patient training, you will have the border collie you want.

Rescue Centers

If you do decide that an adult border collie is right for you, check local and regional rescue centers. These centers take in border collies that have been abandoned or must be placed because of changes in their owner's lives. Other border collies arrive at rescue facilities because the owners have discovered that they are not border collie material. These are dogs in need of homes, some of them desperately so. At rescue

A cow in heat is herded toward the breeding chute by the farm's top hand.

Border collies bring intensity to their work. This tricolored dog appears to be mesmerized by whatever has his attention.

Mountain sheepherders know that when it comes to working stock, one border collie is worth many men.

21

Selecting a single puppy from a litter is not an easy task. If the litter is from good stock and healthy, it really does not matter which puppy you pick.

shelters they are given food, shelter, and as much training and love as possible. Some of the dogs arrive healthy and intact; others, unfortunately, arrive neurotic and fearful of humans. It is the latter group that receives the lion's share of attention and training. Some rescue shelters have had incredible success rehabilitating these animals.

Rescue center personnel will know their dogs intimately. They have a reputation for being extremely honest and will expect the same of applicants for the border collies in their charge. Applications for dogs from rescue shelters are frequently more detailed than those required at dating services and job placement businesses.

A large percentage of the rescue centers have Web pages on the Internet. Most of the information about the rescue organization and border collies currently available will

be available on-line. Again, most of the registries and clubs listed in the back of this book keep close contact with the local border collie rescue centers. They are typically more than happy to provide information about border collie rescue organizations in your area.

Dog or Bitch?

One of the major decisions in selecting a dog of any kind is gender. As in most breeds, there are advantages and disadvantages to both the dog and the bitch. Dogs will tend to be a little larger, more aggressive, more headstrong, and generally more impressive in terms of looks. Bitches are typically smaller, more affectionate, less resistant to training, and a little more sensitive than males.

All the characteristics mentioned in the previous paragraph are tendencies, but, generally, the statements are all true. However, there are female border collies that are bigger than the average male border collie, and some males are shyer and more sensitive than the general run of females.

Before you select a border collie, think about what you really want in a dog. Do you want an affectionate pet that will spend a great deal of time with its head in your lap? Are you easygoing, relatively soft-spoken? Do you have limited space in which to house your border collie? If you answered "Yes" to all, or any of these questions, you might best consider either a female border collie or another breed.

Do you need a strong dog for working stock? Are you loud-spoken or abrupt in your movements? Do you just like the larger, more noble-looking male border collie? If so, consider the male border collie as your first choice.

Again, there is enormous overlap in border collie characteristics. Do not go into the selection process with your decision already made. There is only one thing that is absolute in selecting the sex of your border collie. All border collies should be neutered unless they have been obtained specifically for breeding (see the section on breeding your border collie, beginning on page 90). By neutering your border collie, you will reduce or eliminate many of the problems associated with owning a dog:

• Neutered bitches will not attract suitors every six months and if you want a border collie for working stock, you definitely do not want stray dogs rambling among the herd twice a year. Neutering also eliminates unwanted mixed-breed litters and the resultant drain on the bitch.

• Neutered males will not try to escape from your kennel or yard to go courting. It is likely that more border collie males are killed every year trying to reach a bitch in heat than for any other reason. If your male border collie does not particularly care who is in heat, he will be less likely to go AWOL and wander under the wheels of a moving eighteen wheeler.

• Neutered border collies suffer less from tumors and cancers because their hormone production is reduced.

• The final reason for neutering is to take all but the best border collies out of the gene pool. Border collies with overbites, bad hips, or other defects should be removed from the breeding population when the defect is discovered, no matter what the original reason for purchase.

Working Stock?

One decision you will have to make is whether to obtain a border collie from working stock rather than some other source. The simple answer to this question is "Yes." Border collies became border collies by working. The characteristics of intelligence, athleticism, and willingness to learn have developed as necessary secondary characteristics for the working dog. A border collie from other than working stock will be less likely to have these characteristics to the extent that working stock will. Puppies from farms, ranches, and/or trial stock are preferable over those from stock that has never worked. Be sure that the parents are Orthopedic Foundation for Animals (OFA) certified and have been cleared by a veterinary ophthalmologist. Your chances of getting a healthy, intelligent pup increase dramatically by following these guidelines.

Remember, no matter where you get your border collie, all are high-energy creatures. There is no such thing as a lazy border collie unless it is sick or very old.

Which Pup of the Litter?

If you have set your mind on a border collie puppy and have located a likely litter from working stock, you still have to select a single pup from that litter. That selection is not easy. Healthy border collie puppies are uniformly adorable. At the age of six or eight weeks they tend to be fat, furry, and rambunctious. Selecting one of the litter is akin to selecting the best dish at a great restaurant.

American handlers will frequently give forth the opinion that buyers should select the first puppy that runs up to them. Most buyers will select the friendliest or handsomest pup of a litter, but one of the best-known handlers and trainers of border collies in Britain has suggested that the prospective buyer should take the pup that hangs back to watch. It is his contention that the puppy that sits and observes is the only one of the litter with the brains to know that you are a stranger!

What then is the best way to select a good border collie puppy? There is no best way. If you have found a good,

healthy litter from working stock, just close your eyes and pick a pup.

If you have determined that you need a male or a female, divide the litter by sex and grab a pup from the male or female group. If you really feel that a smooth-haired pup best fits your needs, select a smooth-haired pup. At the age of six to eight weeks there is very little way to tell how a puppy will turn out. Just find a good litter of healthy puppies and pick one.

All healthy border collie puppies are adorable. You will need to use more pragmatic criteria to select your puppy.

As cute as this border collie pup may be, it will require hours of training to reach its true potential.

The Nature of the Border Collie

Intelligence as a Primary Trait

If you ever have the opportunity to examine pictures of the greats of the border collie world, study them closely. Beyond a certain tendency to be long-bodied and long-tailed, they do not look all that much like a single breed. Considering that the winners of major trials are the cream of the breed, how can apparently dissimilar animals comprise a breed? Simple enough: border collies were bred to a functional standard. Rather than breeding for hair coat or bone structure, they were bred to move stock as quietly and efficiently as possible. Intelligent dogs were selected for breeding. All the dogs that win the major trials may not be long-haired nor merled nor white-eyed, but it is almost a certainty that every dog that wins a major trial is exceptionally intelligent, physically sound, and athletic.

This pattern of selection has produced a breed that is recognizable to people who have spent time with them. Newcomers may have to do a double take to be sure that the dog they see is a border collie. Over time, it becomes obvious to everyone involved with the breed that they have more behavioral commonalities than physical ones. A writer for a major English newspaper described border collies as being "unimpressive" when they first came into United Kennel Club conformation competitions. By "unimpressive" he apparently meant that they did not have the high-headed stance, parallel front legs, and heavy coats so typical of the other collie breeds. The writer evidently did not hang around long enough to get to know the breed.

The Herding Instinct

The shepherds and farmers who engineered the border collie's genes wanted a dog they could send out to gather sheep or cattle and bring them back. They succeeded. All border collies have built-in "fetch." "Fetch" is an inbred characteristic of border collies that causes it to move stock around and bring it back to the handler. This characteristic is highly desirable in dogs that work stock, but it can also be troublesome, even dangerous. Lacking anything better to do they will sometimes try to herd whatever they find. Bored or excited border collies, especially young dogs, may try to herd

Border collies will work just about anything that will move, including ducks.

One method of teaching a border collie not to jump up on you is to knee it in the chest when it leaps forward. Care should be taken not to knock the border collie off his feet.

children, joggers, other dogs, or the family cat. Usually this is no more than a nuisance, but problems may arise when the pup begins to nip at the things it is trying to herd. No child likes to be bitten, even if the bite is not serious, and strangers who find a fast-moving dog grabbing at their ankles may not find it amusing. They may, however, find a lawyer.

Excited dogs may also try to herd bicycles, motorcycles, cars, or trucks. Nipping at the front wheel of a moving vehicle has been responsible for the death of innumerable border collies.

Starting as early in their life as possible, young dogs should be trained not to herd anything other than stock. Even then, they should only work on command. When a border collie attempts to "herd" something it should not, it must be corrected as quickly as possible. If, for instance, your border collie tries to bunch the neighbor's children, stop it and shout "*No!*" Any time the behavior occurs again, let the dog know that you

are displeased. It should not take long for it to learn what to work—and when.

Energy Level

A well-known British handler and trainer has claimed that it only takes him 12 miles (19 km) to walk a border collie to the point of exhaustion. The man may well have walked along with the dogs while they ran themselves to exhaustion but there is no way it happened in 12 miles. A point that escapes the handler is that while he may have covered 12 miles, the dog could have matched his one mile (1.61 km) with two or three (3–5 km) of its own.

Border collies frequently have to cover 25 to 45 miles (40–72 km) per day in the course of performing their duties. It is not surprising that the breed is possessed of unbelievable levels of energy. The breed is not as "hyper" as some of the smaller breeds, and it is not characteristic of them to bark aimlessly or to get hysterical at the slightest provocation. However, a border collie that is not given enough exercise or that is constantly confined in a too-small space is more prone than most to go "kennel crazy."

There are other problems that arise from the border collie's high energy level. They are bright and intelligent as well as energetic. If they do not have something to do, they will invent something. If the owner is lucky, the dog will do something that is not destructive. If not, the activity may not be to the owner's liking. Stories about the creativity of the dogs are numerous. One unhappy new owner closed up an 8-week old pup in his bathroom during repairs on his kennels. The next morning he discovered every bit of wallpaper the dog could reach piled neatly in the middle of the floor. While destructive behavior may be characteristic of all breeds of bored puppies, the magnitude of the destruction created by border collie puppies is unique.

Border collies need something to do—and a lot of it.

Exercise

Healthy border collies should be exercised at least once daily. The traditional walk in the park that will provide all the exercise that some breeds need will be a joke to a border collie. Even if you take a pet border collie with you when you run, it probably will not be enough. Most human runners will not even warm up a border collie, unless they happen to be training for marathon competition. Some bicyclists have allowed their dogs to run beside them as they train, with good results. Other, more pragmatic owners have simply loaded their dogs up in a truck and dumped them out on an abandoned road. The dogs then chased the truck for several miles. Of course, in order for this technique to work, the owner must be certain that there will be no other traffic on the road. Logging roads, abandoned mining roads, and hunting trails crisscross much of rural America. Unused roads should be readily available. Even at that, however, the approach is not recommended.

Border Collies in the House

Border Collies can make excellent house pets under the right circumstances. Good grooming is a necessity. In-house dogs should be groomed two or three times a week and baths should also be a weekly occurrence. The breed's thick undercoat can be a nuisance when shed in carpet and on clothes (see Border Collie Care, beginning on page 32).

A border collie's hair is relatively dry and less prone to matting and odor than most breeds, but if it is not groomed regularly, its coat will mat badly. Working border collies are more prone to matting than inside dogs. Outside border collies are exposed to burrs and brambles that can form a

The border collie's working instinct will sometimes cause it to "work" things other than animals.

core around which mats can develop. If the foreign objects are not removed with regular grooming, large mats may form. The longer hair on the tail, on the back of the legs, and the ruff are particularly prone to matting.

Finally, border collies that are kept as house pets should have as much obedience training as possible. Actually, all border collies should have obedience training, but those dogs that live in the house should be under control at all times.

Fortunately, border collies excel at obedience, and training should be quicker and easier than with most breeds. If a qualified obedience instructor is used, training can be particularly quick.

Border Collies on the Farm

Border Collies thrive on the farm. Everything about farm life suits the breed if they are trained and accustomed to moving and controlling stock. The work provides necessary exercise, there is something new to learn every day, and they can be in almost constant contact with their owners.

The border collie's natural athleticism makes it an excellent choice for activities requiring agility.

miles (40 km) day *will* have plenty of energy. If a border collie, particularly a young one, is confined to close quarters, its behavior can go from highly active to completely bizarre.

The real problem with border collies' energy is that they are smart enough to find something to do. Of course, what they find to do may not always be acceptable to their owners. They may dig holes in the yard, chase cats or cars, or even chew up anything they can find. And some dogs with a history of being close-quartered from puppyhood will actually use their energy by pacing like caged tigers.

Well-trained, well-exercised border collies need something to do. Stock work, obedience training, or long runs with a bicycling owner will burn off some of the border collie's energy and help it fit in with the family.

Intelligence: The Positive Aspects, the Negative Aspects

Positive

Owning a smart dog can be a pleasure. Housebreaking a six- or eight-week-old puppy in a few days is definitely more pleasurable than needing six weeks. Watching a dog learn the ins and outs of living with its new family almost overnight can be an amazing experience. Obedience training is faster and much easier with an intelligent dog, if the trainer knows what he or she is doing. The same is true of stock work and learning general good manners. Having an intelligent dog is a blessing. More than one handler has issued a command that would have scattered stock at a critical moment only to have the border collie pause and look back for a correction.

Negative

Now for the downside—border collies with behavior problems are diffi-

However, there are conditions to life on the farm for the border collie. Farm dogs must also be trained. If they are to be stockdogs, they must receive training in that area, as well as obedience training.

How Hyperactive Are They?

Border collies are not hyperactive in the traditional sense of the word. The classic image of a hyper dog includes uncontrolled barking and hysterical behavior. Border collies rarely behave in such a stereotypical hyperactive manner. True, they have a tremendous amount of energy; an animal that is required to run more than 25

cult to correct. Like all intelligent creatures, border collies offer a special challenge when it comes to training. They will learn virtually anything you are willing to teach them. In order to train border collies successfully, you have to be especially consistent and especially quick to reward or correct. There is a saying about puppies from Whitehope Nap bloodlines that the trainer has to be faster and smarter than the puppy. This is true of the entire breed.

The other problem with very intelligent dogs is that they tend to learn things the trainer does not intend. Border collies that have trainers who are slack with them will take advantage of the situation and do as they please. Good dogs that are sold to inexperienced handlers may soon become sloppy in their work. Working border collies will occasionally learn the body language of their handler and anticipate his or her commands—behavior that may cost points in competition. Other border collies may learn when their owners are in a bad mood and refuse to work for them.

Border Collies and Your Possessions

The majority of border collies are outside dogs. The history and nature of the breed has adapted them to living and working outside in all but the most extreme climates. Given the proper attention and training, they can make excellent house dogs but they must be trained from the minute they enter the house or the house can be devastated.

Border collie puppies are like all puppies in some respects: They are furry balls of energy, curiosity, and teeth. If they are not properly trained, everything that can be dragged will be dragged; everything that can be gnawed will be gnawed; everything that can be torn will be torn.

This border collie should be corrected immediately if it is to learn to stay off the furniture.

If you are starting with an older dog, the same basic rules apply: Start the educational process early, be alert, and be consistent. Older dogs are frequently harder to house-train than pups simply because there is more for them to unlearn. Of course, adult dogs

If introduced correctly, border collies will usually get along with other dogs.

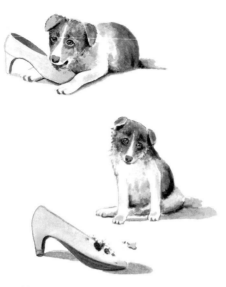

A border collie puppy with nothing to do may discover activities his family will not appreciate.

will not have problems with teething, which could be a definite plus.

First Steps

When the new dog enters the house, it should be shown to its water, food, and bed. If it is to be kept in a crate at night or at times when the owner is out of the house, introduce the dog to the crate (see page 54). The first day or two, its every move should be monitored by the owner or some member of the family. Any time the new dog takes something into its mouth that it should not, the closest family member should remove the object and let the dog know that it has done something wrong. A loud "*No!*" will do the job. If the behavior reoccurs, repeat the correction. Give the dog a few tries to get the point. If it persists, you might escalate the correction to a loud "*No*" combined with shaking it by the scruff of the neck. Do not get too vigorous with the shaking. The point is to get the dog's attention, not to

emulsify its brain. It is all too common for frustrated trainers to lose control and actually hurt their dog. Mother dogs use a similar technique to correct their puppies but they only grip; they do not bite. A well-trained puppy will become a calm, dignified adult that will respect your belongings. The time and effort required to train a new dog will be time and effort well invested.

The Border Collie as a Second Dog

In the environment in which border collies were originally bred all dogs had to earn their keep. They were expected to not bother the stock and to get along with the animals, humans, and other dogs on the farm. As a result, border collies tend to accept new dogs in the house a little better than some other breeds. That is not to say that the owner can impose a new dog on a more established border collie and not expect some difficulties. The resident pet's reaction to a new dog in the house may vary from delight to open aggression. Reaction will vary, largely based on the individual, the age and sex of the individual, and the way the new dog is introduced into the house.

If both the resident dog and the new dog are adult males, expect trouble. There will be a period of time in which dominance is established. Most typically this will involve bluffing, posturing, and a great deal of growling. The resident animal will have the upper hand in the early stages of establishing the relationship. After all, it is his territory. Over time, the personalities of the two dogs will determine dominance.

In some cases, the posturing may give way to fighting. If this occurs, it would be in your interest and that of the dog to keep the dogs separated and introduce them to each other gradually. If the two males continue to fight, try confining the new dog in a crate in the older dog's house. With the new dog in the older dog's territory but protected by the crate, the two males may get used to each other without damage to either. Of course, the two dogs may never come to terms with each other and you will then have to decide what to do with a spare dog.

When a female is introduced into another female's home there is also a chance of trouble. Females will typically establish dominance through the same posturing that males use. There may be growling and raised hackles. The established female may walk stiff-legged around the intruder. The newcomer may adopt a submissive posture and may even roll over on her back to let the more established female know that she is no threat. However, females are not as prone to violence as two males.

Although friction and jealousy can occur when a dog of the opposite sex is introduced into another dog's territory, it is usually minimal. Puppies are usually accepted better than adults since they will submit to virtually anything. If aggression occurs toward pups or females, keep the animals apart.

Problems with Other Pets

Because border collies are unique dogs, they offer unique problems. Around cats or other pets they can be something of a problem and the inbred herding instinct may pop to the surface around cats, ducks, rabbits, or other small animals. Ducks, rabbits, and other pets may be put into some danger if a young dog is allowed to move them around in hot weather.

Some dogs choose to chase cats. This may not seem like much of a threat considering the number of cats chased every day but border collies are a little faster than most breeds of dogs. Even given an exceptional start, most cats will have difficulty escaping from a young, excited border collie. It is rare, however, even when the border collie

Border collies will sometimes try to herd other pets who, needless to say, resent the border collie's efforts.

catches the cat, that any real damage is done; about the only real damage that will be done is to the relationship between you and the cat's owner.

When introducing a young border collie into your home, be certain that someone has an eye on the new dog all the time. If it harms or harasses any of your other pets, it must be corrected immediately. Socialization must begin at once and continue for the dog's life. Once the animal comes to learn that other pets are part of the environment, it will accept them readily.

Most border collies conflicts involve nothing more than bristling and posturing.

Border Collie Care

Border collies are rather easy to care for as their fur is relatively dry and does not tangle easily. This is true of both the smooth- and the rough-haired varieties of the breed. Although the breed is low maintenance, however—at least compared to some other breeds—a regular regimen of grooming is a necessity. Both coat types have a thick undercoat that can become tangled in the presence of dirt, brambles, and twigs.

Basic Equipment for Grooming

The basic hardware requirements for a complete border collie grooming session will include:
- a good pair of scissors
- a metal comb
- a slicker brush
- a pin brush
- a mat rake.

Invest a little extra in these items. Regular grooming, particularly if your border collie is an outside dog, can create a lot of wear and tear on grooming equipment, and cheaper equipment will have to be replaced again and

A top quality brush, comb, pin brush, and pair of scissors will be necessary for a good grooming program.

again. The more expensive grooming equipment will hold up better, sparing you the cost of replacement.

Grooming the Smooth-Haired Border Collie

Smooth-haired dogs have some advantage over their longer-haired brothers and sisters. The absence of "feathers" below the body and around the chest and legs reduces the likelihood that the smooth-haired dog will have mats; grooming three or four times a week will reduce the probability to near zero.

Begin grooming the smooth-haired dog with a pin brush. Start at the side of the dog's head and brush gently toward the tail. Except in cases where the coat is matted, you should be able to cover the entire body with the pin brush without stopping. If you do hit a mat, work around it. It does not do either of you any good to teach the dog that grooming is painful. When you have completed grooming your border collie, use a steel comb to brush the coat against the grain. On a smooth-haired border collie this will not have the impact that it will on the longer-haired variety, but it will remove any hair missed while brushing with the grain.

Mats and tangles: Next, try removing the mats and tangles. The least stressful way to remove mats is to split them with your fingers first. Grab the mat as close to the skin as possible and pull apart gently. If the mat is especially large or compacted, or if it has sticks or briars in the center, it may not split easily. Hold the mat close to the skin with a comb or mat rake and try to pull it apart. Take special care not to hurt your dog. If the border collie becomes edgy or tense, move on to another mat or take a short break. Take your time, move slowly, and try to make the experience as positive as possible for your dog. If the mat proves resistant to fingers and the mat rake, use grooming scissors to split it. Here, again, investing in a good pair of scissors is important. Do not use household scissors; they are too long and their tips can wind up in a dog's eye, or an ear may be shortened by accident. Use the scissors as a last resort.

Try to divide the grooming process into segments. Make brushing separate and distinct from combing. Combing should also be distinguishable from removing mats and tangles. It might help the process if you give your dog a treat between stages.

Grooming the Rough-Haired Border Collie

The only real difference in grooming rough-haired border collies and smooth-haired border collies is that rough-haired dogs have longer guard hairs and "feathers" on the back of their legs and chest. The fine undercoat present in the smooth-haired dogs is also present in their rougher-haired siblings. The longer guard hairs require that the fur be groomed in layers. Longer hair will also mat more readily than smooth hair. Mat removal becomes more important if you own a rough-haired border collie.

Start with the pin brush. Brush from the side of the head to the base of the tail. Work from the side of the head where you originally started, around the head, back to the place where you began. If the fur is especially thick, brush in layers.

When you have successfully brushed the entire surface area of the dog with the grain, use a metal comb.

The easiest way to remove a small mat is to gently pull it apart.

Be cautious while combing and brushing. If you encounter tangles or mats, move around them to come back later. Use the same techniques to remove mats as for smooth-haired dogs. You will find the mat rake even more useful with the rough-haired dogs.

Every effort should be made to make grooming pleasant. Incorporate basic grooming while petting your dog. A pin

Regular grooming is an important part of border collie care.

33

brush may be used to scratch behind a dog's ear as effectively as fingers.

Areas Requiring Special Attention

Teeth

Along with regular physical exams, your border collie should be scheduled for dental exams at least annually. If your veterinarian suggests professional cleaning, have it done. Buildup of tartar on the teeth is the number one cause of tooth disease and loss of teeth. The time and effort involved in getting your dog in for a dental appointment will pay off in the long run.

In between dental appointments:
• Check your pet's teeth regularly for decay, tartar, damage, and inclusions such as wood or other foreign substances.
• Provide veterinary approved chew toys. These toys are designed to enhance canine dental health.
• Feed kibbled foods. Hard foods help reduce plaque buildup on teeth.
• Clean teeth several times a week with brushes and toothpaste especially developed for dogs. Begin clean-

ing your border collie's teeth as early as possible. Make the experience as pleasant as possible. Pull the gums away from the teeth and brush slowly up and down, taking care not to bruise the gums or lips. Work from the back of the mouth to the front, top to bottom. Once the outside of the teeth have been cleaned, use the same techniques to clean the inside. You may find it necessary to take rest periods if your dog gets restless or upset.

Eyes

Beyond genetic problems such as progressive retinal atrophy and collie eye (see page 75), border collies are not especially prone to eye disease. Your pet's eyes may be damaged by external objects or irritated by chemicals or vapors. Every attempt should be made to keep sharp objects and chemical irritants away from the dog's eyes.

Ears

Border collies' ears should be examined regularly since they are particularly attractive to ticks and ear mites. When either of these parasites is found, appropriate treatment should be given (see pages 80–81).

Your border collie's ears should also be examined regularly for damage. While border collies are not as aggressive as some other breeds, they will occasionally get into fights that can produce cuts and abrasions on the ears. They are also extremely active animals and are frequently worked in rough country. Scratches, scrapes, and tears from briars and rough undergrowth are common on the external ears. These wounds should be treated with a local antiseptic. If the wounds are severe, take your dog to a veterinarian for treatment.

The ear canal and underside of the external ear should be cleaned as a regular part of your border collie's grooming. A greasy, sometimes smelly, black substance will build up on the

Clip your dog's nails regularly using a guillotine-style nail clipper. Care should be taken not to cut the quick, or sensitive part of the nail.

inside of the external ear, close to the head. Use a cotton swab to clean the grooves and crevasses of this black matter. Always keep the head of the swab in sight as you clean around the entrance to the ear canal. Dirt from the external ear can be packed into the ear canal, increasing the possibility of ear infection. If you think the ear canal needs to be cleaned, have your veterinarian to take a look at it.

Feet and Nails

Border collies' feet should be examined regularly. Cuts should be treated immediately since they can lead to infections and greater problems. Sharp objects, scrap metal, glass, and other sharp objects should be removed from your pet's environment, and anything that can be done to prevent foot damage should be done.

Border collie pups should have their nails trimmed regularly, beginning at an early age. Special care should be taken with dewclaws. When trimming, stay clear of the quick. The quick is the only part of the nail with nerves and blood vessels. "Quicking" not only produces blood; it hurts. If your border collie associates nail trimming with pain, the next nail trimming session will be extremely difficult, so be careful.

Where Will Your Border Collie Live?

Border collies were meant to live outside. Even though they run to slim builds and relatively little body fat, their dense undercoat makes them all but weatherproof. In fact, they seem to enjoy cold weather. The same temperatures that send humans inside makes them even more energetic. Even so, border collies need a dry, draft-free place of their own.

The Outside Border Collie

The best place to house a border collie is in a well-constructed kennel,

preferably one with a concrete floor and 8 foot (2.45 m) chain-link wire sides. If possible, the kennel should have a secure roof. Border collies are such great climbers and diggers that most standard fencing will not hold them if they decide to go for a walk. If the top of the kennel can-not be enclosed, electric wire should be considered.

Doghouses

A well-constructed doghouse will also be necessary. The best type of house is one that will provide the border collie with a "den," a dark, dry place of its own. The ideal doghouse will be raised off the ground by 3 to 6 inches (7–15 cm), which will prevent the house from being affected by dampness from the soil. The house will also last longer and the border collie will be more comfortable during hot weather. If you have plans to raise puppies in a doghouse, either lower it or provide the puppies with ramps and safety rails.

The house itself should be made with two compartments of equal size that are divided by a wall of heavy

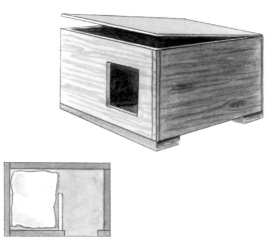

This doghouse provides a warm, draft-proof retreat for the outdoor border collie.

This border collie seems to have lost its car keys.

The best place to put the house is in a covered area. If you are not fortunate enough to have trees over your kennel, consider building a lightweight shed over the entire area.

Keeping a Border Collie in Your Yard

A fenced yard is another good place in which to keep your border collie. If properly built, it will offer some of the benefits of a kennel with more room to move around. Many border collies live happily in a standard chain-link fenced yard, while others do not even slow down when they encounter a 4 foot (1.22 m) chain-link fence. Some will tunnel under fences with the same enthusiasm with which they work sheep or run agility courses. If you plan to keep your border collie in a fenced yard, be sure to have an alternate plan. Consider the practicality of electrifying the bottom and top of your fence. Electric fences are not expensive, are effective if built correctly, and are not all that dangerous. Electric fences also have the benefit of residual effect: Border collies that come to respect a fence will avoid contact with that fence even if it is inactive.

Even those border collies that stay in a fenced yard can offer other problems. The same digging that creates problems with containing the dogs can also create problems in the garden, the yard, and in flower beds. If you happen to catch your border collie digging where it should not, correct it immediately. A loud "*No*" will let it know that it has done something wrong.

Keeping your border collie in the yard presents a number of safety problems. Over time, many homes create hazards that simply do not matter until a dog arrives. Poisonous substances accumulate, wires are frequently used as braces for trellises or trees, and some houses allow border collie puppies access to dangerous areas. Like a house, a yard must be puppy-proofed.

plywood running three quarters the width of the house. One compartment should be accessible from the outside; the other compartment should have only the access provided by the break at the far end of the inside wall.

If you build the house yourself, or if you have it built to your specifications, be certain to secure the roof of the house to the walls with strong hinges. A single piano hinge will serve best and create fewer potential snag points for your dog. While you are designing your dog's house, make certain that the walls, both inside and outside, are easily removable to allow for cleaning.

The size of the doghouse should be determined by the number of border collies you intend to keep in it. Doors should be cut slightly larger than the largest dog to use the house. In cold weather, drape the door opening with a heavy material such as canvas. To make your border collie truly happy, put a broad, covered porch the length of the house.

Take a puppy-level view of your yard and remove any dangers you see.

A border collie that is kept in a fenced yard will still need a "den" of its own. A well-constructed, draft-free doghouse will give your border collie a place to get out of the weather as well as a place to sleep and loaf. If at all possible, put the house in a shady area. Deciduous trees work best as shade for dogs; partial shade is provided in spring and fall, full sunlight is permitted in winter, and full shade in summer.

Border Collies in the House

Keeping border collies in the house poses some of the same problems as keeping them in the yard. First, the house has to be border collie-proofed; potential dangers for your dog will have to be searched out and removed. Remember that, because your dog will have a different point of view regarding your house, literally. An adult border collie's head will be no more than 2 feet (61 cm) off the floor, a puppy's even lower. It will see things that you miss from your vantage point. In your search for electric wires, sharp objects, and potential poisons, sit or lie on the floor. You may feel a little silly, but what you see from your prone position may save your border collie's life.

A Place of Its Own

Your dog will have to have a place of its own. At the very least, it should have an area with a bed and a place to keep its toys. Sam should be taught that the area is his alone. He should also be taught that certain areas of the house are off-limits unless you enjoy border collie hair on your bed and light carpet. If your border collie wanders into forbidden territory, it should be corrected immediately. A few loud "*No*"s will have the new dog dodging couches and detouring around dining rooms.

In order for the restriction training to work, everyone in the house will have to know about it and support it. Punishing the border collie for getting on the couch for days and then having children drag it up there to watch television with them will only confuse the dog. Make sure everyone understands the training plan.

Finally, your border collie needs to be crate-trained if it is to live in your house (see page 54, Crate Training). In fact, *all* border collies should be crate-trained. Inside dogs can use crate training every day, but all dogs should be trained to stay in an air kennel or wire kennel of some sort. Having your dog accustomed to staying in a crate has benefits for both of you: Your border collie gets a safe place to spend its "off" time, and you get a dog that does not mind being closed up in a crate or wire kennel. When you have guests that do not like dogs, or guests that your dog does not like, it may be closed up in its crate for a while. It will also make travel with your dog a great deal easier. Taking a piece of home along with you in the car or the motel room will make your dog more comfortable.

Traveling with Your Border Collie

Millions of miles are logged every year by trainers, handlers, and owners going to and from dog trials and dog shows. Most professionals who travel with dogs in their car enjoy the experience. There is absolutely no reason that you and your border collie cannot enjoy traveling together by automobile, but there are a number of things you must do. The first, and most important, thing you must do is determine whether there are facilities for your border collie at your destination. If not, have a friend care for your pet at home. Better yet, find a good kennel and board your dog for the duration. The second thing is to plan your trip in some detail.

HOW-TO:
Traveling by Automobile

These are a few of the things that you will need when you travel with your dog.

There are a number of things you can do to make an automobile trip with your border collie safe and pleasant:

• Pack a survival kit containing first aid products and medications, including motion sickness medications.

• Never leave your dog alone in a closed car. Even in moderate weather the inside temperature of a closed car can rise to over 100°F (37.8°C), causing your dog to suffer heatstroke and death.

• Never allow your border collie to ride with its head out of the window. It will enjoy the wind in its face, but it is extremely dangerous. Think about the number of times your windshield has been scarred by gravel thrown up by the car in front of you and imagine the damage that same piece of gravel could cause to your pet's eyes. Small pieces of sand and insects can also cause damage to eyes and mucous membranes.

• Always keep your border collie in its crate while the automobile is in motion.

• If you plan to stay overnight in a motel or hotel, call ahead to find accommodations that welcome pets.

• Carry a supply of the food that your dog normally eats. Changing food can result in an upset stomach; the road is pos-

sibly the worst place in the world for a pet to have that problem.

• Schedule your trip so you can stop every hour to exercise your dog. Rest areas along interstate highways usually provide exercise and comfort areas for dogs. Campgrounds and some truck stops provide similar facilities.

• Keep your border collie on its leash when it is out of its crate. Rest areas and motel parking lots may have puddles of

antifreeze, screws, broken glass, and other items that are dangerous to your Border Collie.

• Keep your border collie in its crate in the motel or hotel room.

• Have your dog up to date on all inoculations. If you plan to cross international boundaries, have a valid health certificate with you.

• Pack your border collie's chew toys, favorite towel or blanket, and anything else that might make it feel at home.

Traveling by automobile with your border collie can be pleasant if it is well planned.

Plan travel with your border collie around hourly relief stops.

Traveling by Air

Unless you are moving or taking your border collie to a trial, arrange to leave it at home. If you must take the dog with you on a plane, take the following steps:

• Buy or rent an airline-approved air kennel. If you already have one, you are one step ahead. Some airlines rent air kennels.

• Make sure your air kennel is in good working order. Most air kennels have two halves that are held together with machine screws and wing nuts. Be sure that all of the screws and nuts are in place and tight. Also make sure that hinges and latches work as they should. If your kennel has an adapter for a water dish, be sure that it is attached and in good condition.

• Get all inoculations and health certificates required by the airlines. Most airlines require that health certificates be issued no more than ten days prior to departure.

• Leave from an airline hub. If you can arrange it, try to get a direct flight from a hub. More pets are lost in the exchange at connecting airports than anywhere else. The most common problem with pets and air travel is that they do not make connecting flights. Eventually, the misplaced pets will be put on an airplane to your final destination. Even at that, the stress and inconvenience caused by a pet missing a flight is worth the extra effort of departing from a hub city.

• Insist on watching your border collie being put on the same airplane you are taking. Some airline personnel will try to reassure you that your dog will make the flight and that you should not worry—go ahead and worry. Stand your ground. If the airline will not allow you to watch your border collie being put on board, change airlines.

If you must travel by air with your border collie, arrive early and watch your dog as it is being loaded.

• Arrive early. You and your pet should get to the airline check-in counter at least two hours before departure. Getting there an extra half hour early will help offset any of the standard delays and problems normally encountered getting to airports.

• If your border collie is frightened of loud noise or strange people, talk to your veterinarian about using tranquilizers for the flight. Current veterinary wisdom advises against using tranquilizers at high altitude but your veterinarian will know what is best for your border collie.

• Make sure your border collie has water in the on-door adapter. Water will survive handling better and last longer if it is put into the adapter and frozen before the adapter is attached to the crate.

• If your border collie is coming off an illness or surgery, talk to your veterinarian about the advisability of taking it along. The same goes for old or very young border collies.

HOW-TO:
Puppy-Proofing Your Home

When puppy-proofing the home, a survey of the house should be done from the puppy's level.

Border collie puppies present a special challenge in making your house safe for them. Certainly, some terriers are as active as border collies but no breed combines the energy and the intelligence that comes with the border collie breed. It is relatively easy to train a border collie puppy to avoid certain areas of your house. First, you must decide what areas are dangerous for your pet and make it stick. Border collie puppies will find things you did not know you had, get into places you never thought they could, and chew virtually everything they find.

Checking Out Potential Dangers

Do not let your experiences with other breeds fool you into thinking that you have a handle on border collie safety. Border collies think differently than other breeds. If you are to keep one in your house, you will have to start from scratch to make it safe:
• Play puppy. Get down on your hands and knees, or on your stomach if the puppy is very young. Look for anything threatening that might catch your eye from that angle.
• Check for objects that may lodge in your puppy's throat or otherwise cause it damage. You might be surprised at the number of coins, pins, beads, and other small items you can find in puppy-accessible areas of

your home. As you approach holiday seasons that traditionally involve decorations, repeat your check to be sure that your decorations have not provided more dangerous fodder for your border collie.
• If you live in an older home, even one that has been completely redecorated, check for lead-based paints. Border collie puppies are world-class gnawers. If there are patches of lead-based paints around, even under safer types of paint, take steps to remove it. Lead-based paints are every bit as danger-

ous to puppies as they are to human children.
• Check for the presence of electrical cords. Border collie puppies will gnaw anything—electrical extension cords are not only attractive to puppies; they can be fatal.
• Check your house for toxic plants. Remove plants that may harm your puppy. See the shaded box for some of the potentially dangerous plants you may encounter. Plants will vary from area to area. It would be a good idea to check with your county extension agent for a

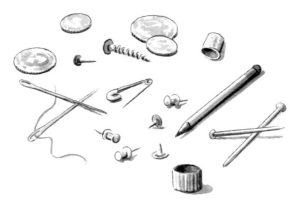

Any object small enough for a puppy to swallow can be dangerous. One step in puppy-proofing a home is removing all potentially dangerous items from the puppy's reach.

Potentially Dangerous Plants

Atamasco Lily
Bitter Sneezeweed
Black Cherry
Black Locust
Black Nightshade
Bladderpod
Bracken Fern
Buckeye
Buttercup
Castor Bean
Cherry Laurel
Chinaberry
Choke Cherry
Cocklebur
Coffee Senna
Common Buttonbush
Common Cocklebur
Common Sneezeweed
Common Yarrow
Crotolaria
Eastern Baccharis
Fetterbush
Great Laurel
Hairy Vetch
Hemp Dogbane
Horsenettle
Jimsonweed
Johnsongrass
Lantana

Leucothoe catesbaei
Maleberry
Mexican Poppy
Milkweed
Mountain Laurel
Mustard
Oleander
Perilla Mint
Poison Hemlock
Poison Ivy
Poison Oak
Poison Sumac
Pokeberry
Rattlebox
Red Buckeye
Redroot Pigweed
Rosebay
Sesbania
Scotch Broom
Sheep Laurel
Showy Crotalaria
Sicklepod
Spotted Water Hemlock
St. John's Wort
Stagger Grass
Sweet Clover
Sweetshrub
White Snakeroot
Yellow Jessamine

more detailed list. Please understand that the toxicity of the listed plants varies greatly. Some of the plants will cause only minor stomach upset; others will cause sudden death.

• If you have to have a toxic material in your home, be sure that your border collie is closed out of the rooms or areas that have the toxic products. Roach and rat poisons are materials that you may have to use from time to time. Paint thinners and some types of paints also have toxic materials as components. Read the labels of such products and take steps to protect your dog.

• Check for places that your puppy might get into but might not be able to get out of. Areas behind appliances and heavy furniture provide intriguing places for exploration but they can also be traps for your puppy. Shove things closer to the wall or rearrange other furniture to close off problem areas.

• If your home is multistory, close off areas that would allow the puppy to leap or fall far enough to hurt itself. If you have a balcony, be doubly careful about allowing the puppy access. Make sure that railings will not allow the pup to get its head stuck in a gap.

• If your border collie has access to the areas where you keep your automobiles, learn to check for its presence every time you drive in or out. Before you leave, walk around the car making certain that there is not a puppy asleep under a wheel or hiding under the car. It is a good practice to start a "family check" before getting into the car. That simply requires that the individual driving the car asks other members of the family, "Where's Joe?" or "Is Mist in her crate?" If you live alone or if the whole family will be gone, put Sam in his crate before you start your car.

While most of these puppy-proofing procedures may seem obvious, taking such simple steps may save your puppy's life.

Activities for Your Border Collie

Aside from having a surprisingly high level of intelligence, a relatively long body, long tail, and long legs, border collies are a highly variable breed. They vary in temperament from bold and aggressive to "soft," shy, and retiring. Size varies as much as temperament. There are very few absolutes relating to border collies, but the one thing that is absolute is this: Border collies must have something to do. Those that are taken into homes that provide every other need except for a special activity may become neurotic, destructive, or unpredictable.

It really does not matter what a border collie is given to do, as long as there is something. Before buying or accepting a border collie into your life, have plans to include some activity along with the dog.

Trialing

Over the last 20 years or so, the number of stock dog trials has increased dramatically. These trials bring out the best in the breed, as well as providing exercise for the dog and the handler. On just about any weekend during the spring, early summer, and fall, a stock dog trial is taking place within driving distance of your home. The trials are sanctioned, sponsored or even put on by state, local, or national border collie associations. Rules for the trials are standardized around the trial rules put forward by the International Sheep Dog Society, although American courses tend to be somewhat shorter.

Trialing is a hobby that requires three things: time, effort, and patience. A good dog helps, too. Dogs may be obtained already trained or they may be trained from scratch. Either way, trial dogs must be worked daily and trained constantly. It is axiomatic on the trial circuit that trials are won at home, not on the trial course. What this means, of course, is that handler cannot expect more of the dog than the dog knows how to give. If the handlers allow sloppy work on a daily basis, they can expect exactly the same thing on the trial course.

Trial courses in the United States will range from 300 to 440 yards (274–402 m), a few longer. In Great Britain, trial courses may run to 800 yards (732 m).

There are typically three classes in American stock trials: Professional, Pro-Novice, and Novice-Novice.

The Professional category is for handlers and dogs that have won three or more Novice classes.

Pro-Novice is for experienced handlers and border collies that have won less than three Novice classes.

Novice-Novice is for the inexperienced handler and dog.

Classifications will vary according to the organization sponsoring the trials.

Sheep trials will require that the dog be sent out on command to gather the sheep. Ultimately, the dog and handler will be required to bring the sheep around the handler, drive them through two freestanding gates, and pen them. Most trials will require that one or more sheep be "shed" or cut out of the flock.

Novice classes typically only require the sheep to be fetched and penned over shorter courses. Cattle trials are typically simpler than sheep trials. Cattle must be fetched and penned over a shorter course.

The AKC Herding Program

The American Kennel Club sponsors a herding program for a number of herding breeds, including the border collie. The program is divided into two classifications: Testing and Trial.

The Test classification offers two titles: Herding Test Dog (HT) and Pre-Trial Tested Dog (PT). In order to qualify for the Herding Test Dog, the dog simply has to show some inherent ability to herd stock and some degree of trainability. The Pre-Trial Tested Dog has some training and can move stock over a simple course.

The Trial classification has four titles. Herding Started (HS), Herding Intermediate (HI), and Herding Excellent (HX) are the three progressively more difficult titles. After a border collie earns the HX it can then work toward accumulating 15 Championship points and the Herding Championship (HCH).

Other Trials

Trials based on ISDS rules differ from American Kennel Club herding events in that they are purely competitions. Titles are given only to winners of specific events and then for only one year.

To be competitive at border collie trials, you will need;
• a border collie from good stock
• a place to train your dog
• stock to use in training
• some training for yourself

Most of the better handlers and dogs at stock dog trials are farmers, ranchers, or people who work their dogs with stock every day. The best trial dogs are also the best everyday work-

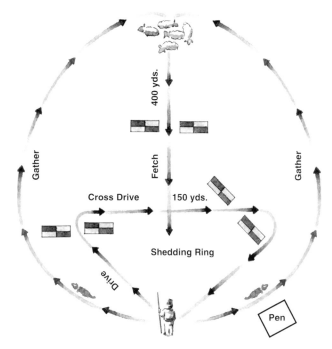

The course most commonly used in sheepdog competitions is between 300 and 400 yards in length.

ing dogs. If you intend to compete and intend to have the competition mean anything, plan to spend hours every day practicing and training your border collie. Trialing provides all the purpose and exercise of farm work along with the opportunity to meet and socialize with some truly fine people.

Obedience

Anyone who has ever worked with a number of different breeds of dogs knows that a breed's receptiveness to training is, in part, determined by its original purpose. Herd guardian breeds are naturally independent and more difficult to train. In the world of obedience, border collies have an unfair advantage. They have been selected and bred for intelligence and willingness

43

Reward and attention are important to any border collie training program.

A border collie and her handler wait at the stake for their turn in a sheep herding trial.

to learn and to follow directions. In recent years these characteristics have enabled them to become one of the most dominant breeds in obedience and it is unusual to attend an obedience competition in which they do not place. The level of their dominance is limited by the number of border collies entered and the quality of the trainers.

Obedience is the ideal outlet for the border collie owner who either does not have the means to train a dog for working stock or the interest to do so. A well-trained dog will receive the attention and exercise it needs during training and competition. The levels and types of obedience competitions and titles available offer exercise and competition for an extended period of time. Most owners find obedience an excellent outlet for their border collies. At the very least, all dogs should finish training that would qualify them for a CD certificate. The CD (companion dog) level of obedience training requires that the dog work at heel, sit, down, stay, and come on command. While the benefits of all the requirements may not be obvious, each is critical for a well-mannered dog.

The early stages of obedience training are probably more strenuous for the owner than for the border collie. Just downing, coming, heeling, and staying do not burn up a large percentage of a border collie's energy. The exercise attained in the early classes should be augmented with some other form of physical exercise until the border collie begins work on its tracking or Shutzhund certificate. In the mean time, the discipline and control imposed during CD and CDX (Companion Dog Excellent) levels of training will make your border collie an easier animal with which to live. See the section on obedience training for more detail about the various obedience titles (page 52).

After a dog receives a CD or Companion Dog certificate, it can still compete for years, pursuing increasingly difficult certificates. It should be pointed out that the CD is not easily achieved. It requires hours of training, at least one class from a qualified obedience trainer. The trained dog must then compete in at least three American Kennel Club-approved obedience trials and score 170 out of the 200 points possible. In each of the trials in which the competitor scores a total of 170 points, it must also score at least 50 percent in all segments of the trial. Very few dogs receive their CD after only three trials. It can be a time-consuming process, even for a border collie.

Border collies are currently the breed ranked tops in trainability intelligence. The number one obedience dog of all-time of all breeds was Obedience Trial Champion (OTCH) Heelalong's Chimney Sweep, a border collie.

A young black-and-white border collie performs his long down while other competitors wait their turn.

Frisbee

Chasing and catching a Frisbee is something that comes easily to many border collies. Calm, confident border collies will see the disk in the air and become intrigued by this new mystery; others will be indifferent and, unless they are actually struck with the Frisbee, they will pretty much ignore it. The disinterested dogs will sit and watch you throw the Frisbee until your arm is numb, while some will take the fact that you have thrown a Frisbee in their direction as a reprimand. These dogs will slink off or run away from you and the disk. If this happens, consider another activity.

If your border collie will play "fetch," it has potential as a Frisbee dog. Instead of throwing a stick or ball for it to retrieve, throw a Frisbee. Throw it close to the border collie after getting it excited, using the same words you use to get it excited about fetching its stick or ball. If the dog retrieves the Frisbee, or even walks over to where it has fallen, be lavish with your praise.

Throw the Frisbee again, just a little farther than the first throw. If your border collie retrieves faster or improves its performance at all, praise it lavishly. Over time, the border collie will learn that catching the Frisbee in the air is more exciting than retrieving it from the ground. With practice, it can execute all the moves you have seen performed on television.

The speed of the breed is obvious in this border collie's outrun.

The Frisbee provides an excellent form of exercise for border collies. Care should be taken to avoid putting the dog in a position that could cause it to land awkwardly. Such landings can result in severe injury.

For the border collies that take to the Frisbee, it is an excellent form of exercise. It also has the benefit of being relatively inexpensive. Maintenance and upkeep on frisbees are much less costly than on sheep or cattle. Border collies can be exercised in a relatively limited area with a Frisbee. It only requires a park or small field to throw the disk. If your dog is adept enough, there are local and national competitions, and if your border collie is especially good, one of the national dog food companies sponsors a team of border collies that tours and puts on Frisbee demonstrations. Your dog might just qualify for professional status!

A note of caution: Border collies are highly athletic and highly competitive. If they are interested in catching the Frisbee, they will go to great lengths to come down with one thrown in their direction. High leaps and spins in the air are common in this sport. Problems may arise when a dog spins in the air, lands off balance, and injures itself. Care should be taken to throw the Frisbee so that it can be caught, and in such a way that the border collie can land safely. Young dogs should not have their physical abilities overtaxed. When starting out, keep the Frisbee close to the ground. Concentrate on distance rather than height with younger dogs. It is also important that you work with one of the softer Frisbees made especially for dogs in order to prevent a great deal of the tooth damage that can occur with Frisbees made for humans.

Flyball

Flyball, a bizarre sport invented in California in the 1970s, has very little to do with anything except a good time. The actual competition of flyball requires at least two teams of four dogs each. There is a course, 51 feet (15.5 m) in length. The first of four hurdles is 6 feet (1.8 m) from the starting line. Hurdles are spaced 10 feet (3 m) apart. Fifteen feet (4.6 m) past the last hurdle is a spring-loaded box.

The object of the competition is for the first dog to go over the hurdles to the box. When the dog presses the top of the box, a tennis ball is shot upwards. The dog is supposed to catch the ball and return to the finish line, over the hurdles. When the first dog crosses the finish line, the second dog can go. The first team to have all four members complete without errors wins.

Flyball is fun and does provide some exercise. It is a way for the owner and the border collie to spend time together. It will not provide all the exercise required for an adult border collie, however, some other form of exercise will have to be provided.

Like trialing, flyball may be pursued at any number of levels, from local fun competitions all the way to the national level. It, too, provides the opportunity to spend time with the dogs and with the people who love them.

Tracking

The activity of tracking is pretty much what the name implies: A dog is trained to follow a scent trail. The activity is a natural for all dogs. Their highly developed sense of smell makes olfactory input as important as any other sense. Even breeds not normally associated with tracking can do well.

The American Kennel Club offers three titles in the tracking category:

1. Dogs that successfully complete a basic test may have the title Tracking Dog (TD) placed after their name.

2. Completion of a more difficult and advanced test gives them the right to use Tracking Dog Excellent (TDX).

3. The Variable Surface Tracking Test (VST) is an even more difficult test over a number of different type of surfaces. The dog may be asked to follow a trail over grass, pavement, concrete, and/or dirt.

Once a dog has earned its TD, TDX, and VST, it may use the title Champion Tracker (CT).

Agility

Agility began as something to fill breaks during jumping horse competitions. Agility competition is a timed event over a course that looks remarkably like a miniature horse jumping course with some additional obstacles added. Dogs will be asked to go over hurdles, climb ramps, crawl through pipes, walk along rails, and run through "weave poles," a slalomlike arrangement of poles. The competitors are required to run the course in a prescribed order, with a given starting and ending point. The dog that completes the course with the lowest time and the fewest faults wins. Faults are awarded by judges for not taking an obstacle cleanly.

Every agility trial is potentially different from every other trial. Even second and third runs may differ in the course layout and/or the order of the obstacles. Obviously, the critical aspects of agility training are training and communication between dog and handler. As extra incentive, border collies that are registered with the American Kennel Club can compete for titles in agility, earning the following titles: Novice Agility (NA), Open Agility (OA), Agility Excellent (AX), and Master Agility Excellent (MX).

Border collies do exceptionally well in agility competitions due to their natural athleticism, intelligence, and trainability.

Scent Hurdles

This is another strange sport. Basically, a variation on flyball, it uses the same course size, the same hurdles, and rules for hurdles. The difference is that there are four balls, one of which has been scented by the dog's trainer. The idea is for the dog to get over the hurdles, select the correct ball, and return to the finish line. Scent hurdles add an interesting twist to an already fun activity.

Like flyball, this is an enjoyable activity at which border collies can excel. Unfortunately, scent hurdles will not provide enough exercise for the normal, healthy border collie and should be augmented with more strenuous exercise.

Other Activities

There are literally thousands of activities over and beyond those listed above. Trying to list all the activities a border collie and its owner can participate in would be a monumental task. There are, however, a few things that do catch the attention.

Water Activities

As a group, border collies love the water. If one is fortunate enough to have access to water, it will probably spend a great deal of its time swimming. Swimming is an ideal recreation for border collies in warmer areas or

Agility competition is not only a natural fit for the border collie, it is an excellent form of exercise.

Flyball is another way to burn off some of your border collie's energy.

A border collie shows its agility over hurdles on the way to the flyball machine.

during the warm months of the year. Your border collie can exercise as much as it needs to without fear of heat exhaustion or stroke. A family with children will appreciate the border collie's love of water. However, care should be taken when a border collie spends a great deal of time in, or around, water.

Its dense undercoat holds water close to the skin and in hot, damp areas, the border collie can develop fungus infections and other skin diseases. If you live in such an area, be sure that you monitor your border collie's skin condition. At the first sign of fungus or, "hot spots," get it to a veterinarian for treatment. It

A border collie and corgi cool of in a small pool of water.

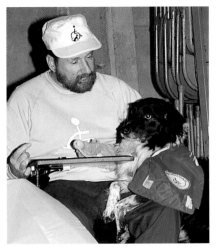

A service dog trainee returns a dropped umbrella to the trainer.

may be necessary to limit your dog's access to water in order to minimize skin problems. Border collies that have ready access to water may also develop ear problems.

Sledding

In colder areas of the country, border collies have been used in sled teams. Admittedly, they were not bred to pull loads, but their intelligence and energy has made them valuable members of dog teams, especially as lead dogs.

In addition to all the activities listed above, border collies have also been used in rescue work, as drug-sniffing dogs, and deaf aid dogs, as well as in Schutzhund work, a difficult combination of obedience, tracking, agility, and protection although most border collies are not aggressive enough for the protection part of Schutzhund work.

Flyball competitors take a breather after their turns.

This border collie easily performs the difficult task of moving nervous sheep down a noisy street.

With its dense double coat, the border collie is well suited for winter sports.

Training

Why Is It Necessary?

With the possible exception of fingernails on a chalkboard, there are few things in life more irritating than an out-of-control dog. Most out-of-control dogs get that way from lack of training and discipline. Well-trained dogs, no matter what breed, are typically a pleasure to be around. Border collie owners and trainers do have a certain advantage over other dog owners since their dogs are easier to train, but, of course, untrained border collies are no more pleasant to be around than any other breed. Not only will some minimum level of training make your border collie more pleasant to be with, it could literally save its life.

One border collie owner tells the story of his first border collie. The dog was only three or four months old but the owner had already taught him to

Border collies should be corrected immediately when they violate the "house rules."

down, come, and *stay.* The pup was raised as a house dog and had little experience outside his own backyard. One afternoon, while the border collie's owner was away from home, the owner's wife answered the front door bell. The puppy, excited by the presence of a stranger, ran out the door and toward a busy street. With no other options, the wife yelled, "*Down!*" as loudly as she could. The runaway puppy dropped as if it had been shot, about 6 inches (15 cm) from the pavement. Not only had training put the pup under control, it had probably saved his life.

Various Approaches to Training

In the course of trying to train your border collie, you will come across as many different training styles as there are trainers. You will be presented with raw behavior modification where every desired behavior is rewarded or "reinforced" and every undesirable behavior is punished. Other approaches take advantage of the "alpha male" behavior inherent in all dogs.

It is very easy to become distracted by the variety of techniques and philosophies in use. If you are inexperienced at training dogs, your best bet is to locate as many amateur and professional trainers as you can find and pick their brains. You will probably be surprised at how willing dog people are to talk about how they do things. You may even want to sit in on a few basic obedience classes. After all this you will certainly find a training technique, or a set of training techniques, that will suit you best. There are all manner of trainers using a wide variety of training methods with a great deal of success. The only commonalities you will find will be consistency, willingness to perform the same training procedures over and over, and the use of correction rather than punishment. Pick and choose among the techniques until you get the results you want. The truth is, it does not matter what training technique you use as long as it works.

The techniques presented in this chapter are not based on any belief that they are the only way to approach that type of training, but because they have been proven to work.

All the training approaches have one thing in common: They view the border collie's entire life as a training session. Every time a dog is worked, every time it is run through its paces, it is in a learning situation. If it is allowed to be sloppy in accepting commands, it will become sloppy. If it is held close to its commands, it will work as it has been trained. Moreover, every time a border collie is worked, the handler can zero in on problems and weaknesses that the dog may have.

Minimum Command Sets

All dogs that will interact with strangers should have complete Companion Dog (CD) training. This training teaches a dog to walk at heel, to sit, to down, to stay for extended periods, and to come on command. Some owners will not see the benefit of all the commands, but every command in CD training exists because it makes the dog easier and more pleasant to live with.

At a minimum, all dogs should be trained to down and come. Both commands should be honored immediately, not when the dog gets around to it. The *down* command gives the owner some level of control over his

or her dog. If the dog will stop immediately and fall to its stomach, the owner can keep the dog from potential danger or from annoying others. The benefit of the *come* command is obvious. The time, energy, and irritation saved by having a dog come when called makes the training worthwhile.

Housebreaking

The easiest way to housebreak a pup is simply never to give it the opportunity to defecate or urinate in the house. Your job as the trainer is to make it easy for the pup to go outside regularly and often. Try to schedule the puppy's arrival at your home at the beginning of a long weekend or a vacation when someone will be around the puppy at all times. Do not bring a new puppy into your home when you expect a lot of visitors. Christmas, Thanksgiving, and other family holidays will generally have too much commotion in your home for the puppy to be introduced successfully.

There are a couple of tricks you might use to make housebreaking a little easier. Take an old towel to the

Puppies should be provided with a special place to eliminate. They should be taken to the spot after meals, first thing in the morning, and just before being put up for the night.

breeders and have them put it in with the puppies; then retrieve the blanket and place it in your new border collie's crate. The odor of the litter and the pup's mother will help identify the crate as being home. This will not only help prevent the puppy from fouling the crate, but will make the transition from breeder to your home easier.

The other, and less pleasant, thing you can do is to sack up some droppings or straw upon which the puppy or its siblings have relieved themselves. Put this scented "bait" in an area where you would prefer the pup to do its business. By "salting the mine" in this manner, you have created a spot the pup automatically associates with its natural functions. The day you bring the puppy home, stop by this preselected spot and let it relieve itself before you take it into the house. Do not just put it down and expect him to go as if it were on command. Give it a few minutes to do the normal sniffing and site selection that all dogs do. Be prepared to wait a while for the pup to find the perfect spot. After it has gone, the chance of its fouling your house is reduced and the site is further marked as an acceptable spot for such activities.

When you finally take the new pup inside, make sure that there will be someone available to monitor its activities at all times. At the first sign of restlessness or whimpering, take the pup out to its spot and wait. Better yet, have regularly scheduled trips outside. One trip should be the first thing in the morning; others should be planned for after meals. There should always be an extended trip before you and your family go to bed. Remember, there can never be too many trips for a young puppy.

You should understand that there will probably be accidents. No matter how fast the puppy progresses, changes in food or the onset of sickness can cause the puppy to foul your carpet or tile. If this happens, do not waste your time scolding the puppy. Clean the floor with deodorizing cleanser and let it dry before you let the puppy back into the area. By deodorizing the area, you will prevent the pup from making the association with your carpet and bowel movements.

Punishment should *never* be used in housebreaking. The practice of rubbing a puppy's nose in its mistakes is a definite waste of time—all you will have after a few such episodes is a smelly puppy that avoids you.

Obedience Training

Levels
There are three levels of competition in basic obedience: Novice, Open, and Utility. If these levels of competition are pursued, they can result in Companion Dog (CD), Companion Dog Excellent (CDX), and Utility Dog (UD) titles, respectively.

Exercises
There are six exercises in Novice class:
1. Heel on leash
2. Stand for examination
3. Heel off leash

A border collie moves in on a small flock of sheep.

4. Recall
5. Long sit
6. Long down
   Open work includes:
1. Heel off leash
2. Long sit
3. Long down
4. Down on recall
5. Stand for examination
6. Retrieve on the flat
7. Retrieve over the high jump
8. Broad jump
   Utility level work includes:
1. Signal exercise
2. Directed jumping
3. Directed retrieve
4. Two scent discrimination tests

Scores

The American Kennel Club scores all obedience competitions levels the same. A perfect score in Novice, Open, and Utility competitions is 200. In order to earn any of the obedience titles, a competitor must earn a minimum of 170 points in three competitions. Successful completion of a competition is referred to as "earning a leg." Even with a score of 170 or more points, earning a leg requires that at least 50 percent of possible points must be scored on all exercises. A competitor cannot specialize in recall or drop on command and completely blow the heeling exercises. A dog competing in obedience must be competent in all exercises if it is to get a "leg." With three legs, a Novice dog earns its Companion Dog certificate, an open competitor earns a Companion Dog Excellent certificate, and a contestant in the Utility class will pick up its Utility Dog diploma.

After earning its Utility Dog (UD) certificate, obedience competitors can attempt to earn points toward an Obedience Trial Championship (OTCH). Competitors can earn points toward an OTCH by placing first or second in an Open B or Utility Class. If the Utility Class is divided, only Utility B qualifies.

In order to become an Obedience Trial Champion, a competitor must win 100 points in competition to include:

- A first place in Utility (Utility B, if divided) with three dogs competing.
- A first place in Open B with at least six dogs in competition.
- Another first in either of the two classes mentioned above, under the same conditions.

The three firsts must be earned under three different judges.

Where to Get Obedience Training for Your Border Collie

If you do not know someone who can recommend a good obedience trainer, there are several alternative sources of information. First, try contacting the kennel club in your area. If you cannot find the local kennel club in your yellow pages, wait for a while—kennel clubs advertise bench and obedience events long before they occur. By reading your local newspaper you should have ample notification of upcoming obedience trials. Most advertisements will include a number for registration that you can call to ask for a list of obedience trainers. If the local club keeps such information, they are typically more than eager to pass on such lists. As a rule, though, clubs will not provide recommendations.

If you can get a list, pick someone close to where you live and visit one or two of the classes. If you like the trainer and the trainer's methods, sign up for the next class. If the trainer turns out to be unacceptable, find the next closest class and spend some time watching that trainer. It should not take more than a class or two before you find a trainer who suits your needs.

If you cannot come up with any leads locally, try calling or writing to the American Kennel Club. They will have a list of all obedience trials in your area as well as clubs and organizations that might be able to help you.

HOW-TO:
Crate Training

One of the first purchases you should make if you intend to keep your border collie in the home is a wire crate, or well-built plastic carrier. Crate-train him using the steps discussed below. Later, when it is necessary to take the pup to the veterinarian or to travel with it, the crate will be familiar and comforting. Also, when it is necessary to confine the young dog for any length of time, there will be no problem getting it into the crate.

Crate training is critical for the inside border collie.

- Take your border collie out for an extended period before shutting it up for the night. Be sure that it has eliminated before you bring it back inside. Do not be in a hurry.
- Place the crate in a spot where the pup can see family activities but where there is some peace and quiet. Also, the crate should be in a spot that does not get blasted by cold drafts when a door is opened, and should not be directly in front of a heating vent or in direct sunlight during the summer. Find a place where *you* would be comfortable and put the crate there.
- Buy a crate that your pup can grow into. Do not buy a puppy-sized crate that will have to be replaced as the pup grows.
- Buy the best crate or wire kennel you can afford. If necessary, you can partition the crate into sections using lightweight plywood. Partitioning the crate will prevent the puppy from dividing it for its own purposes—sleep on one side, relief on the other.
- Before you put a young dog in the crate for the night, do what you can to burn up its excess energy. If you have children, let them play with the puppy but make sure they understand that roughhousing is not allowed; the object is to tire the pup, not harm it.
- When the puppy is free in the house, leave the door of the crate open. This will allow the puppy to return to the crate for a nap or just to rest. Over time, the puppy will come to associate the crate with safety and quiet.
- If you have more than one dog, be sure to have enough crates to go around. Do not try to get by with fewer crates than you have dogs.
- Make certain that your puppy has something to entertain itself while it is awake. Keep one of its toys and a chewy in its cage but do not put so much in its crate that it has no room to stretch out.
- Do not feed or water your pup in the crate. It needs to understand that it will be fed in the same place all the time, and that the crate is *not* that place.
- Once the puppy is closed in for the night, do not remove it from the crate. Responding to its whimpers and whines will only increase them.
- If the puppy makes noise after being confined, try to quiet it by speaking sternly. Physical punishment will not work. In order to punish the puppy you will have to take it out of the crate and it will therefore be rewarded for making noise. By the time you get the pup out of the crate, it will be confused about its punishment: Is it being punished for the noise it was making, the noise the crate made when the door opened, or the noise you may have made?
- Get up in the morning at your normal time. Do not change your schedule for the puppy.

No matter how much noise it makes, never remove your puppy from its crate once it has been settled for the night.

Minimum Equipment Needed for Obedience Training

Leads: To get started in obedience training you will need a 6-foot (1.8 meter) lead. Choose a well-made, 1-inch-wide (2.5 cm) lead made of leather or nylon. Some obedience trainers prefer a shorter lead but 6 feet is recommended. Be sure that the snap is well made and of heavy stainless steel or brass; lightweight snaps will not last long with the wear they will receive. The "handle" or loop at the end opposite the snap should be double-stitched. If you take your border collie to an obedience class, your teacher will be able to point you toward a good source for leads and other equipment.

Collars: You will also need a sturdy training collar. These collars are most commonly referred to as "choke collars." Training collars are not used to restrict air intake in the trainee, but to correct the dog when it does not respond immediately to a command. *The training collar should not be left on after training sessions.* A good leather or nylon buckle collar should be used for the dog's walks and restraining it under normal conditions.

You will find that training collars are available in a variety of sizes and qualities. Buy the heaviest, best-made collar you can afford. You will not need one of the training collars with spikes on the inside; border collies learn quickly that such a collar is painful. They will also learn that obedience sessions are to be avoided if you use such a collar. Stick to the standard stainless steel or chrome collar in the correct weight for your border collie.

Remember when you put the training collar on your border collie that there is a right and wrong way to perform this simple task. The collar will have a ring at each end. A loop is formed with the collar by looping it through one of the rings. One ring will have the chain of

Although it may seem like a small thing, it is important that the training collar be put on correctly.

the collar passing through it; the other will be clear. It is the ring through which no chain passes that should have the leash attached to it. The free ring should be placed to the right side of the border collie's neck.

While all of this may sound somewhat picky, putting the training collar on backward can cause the collar to not release correctly. Not only can this be dangerous, but choking a dog, even briefly, can sour it on training.

An issue you may encounter is whether or not to use rewards other than verbal ones. Although you may hear passionate arguments against using tidbits to reinforce a desired behavior, there is no real reason not to. You will be told that once you begin to use snacks as rewards, you will have to use rewards forever. This is just not true. It is not necessary to reward a behavior every time it occurs once the association is made, but punishment must occur *every time* there is an undesirable behavior.

A training collar is an important piece of equipment, but it should always be removed when not in use.

Basic Commands

Try to make the training sessions fun. Encourage your pet and use praise freely. The training collar should only be used to keep its head up in the early stages of training. Do not forget that it is young and inexperienced. If you lose your temper and jerk the young dog around, it may sour on training all together. Finally, keep the sessions brief. A 15-minute training period is more than enough in the beginning.

Sit

You will not actually be teaching your border collie to sit. Except in extreme cases of hip dysplasia, border collies sit as a normal part of their behavior. It will be your job to teach it when and where to sit.

Before you begin training, put the training collar on your border collie

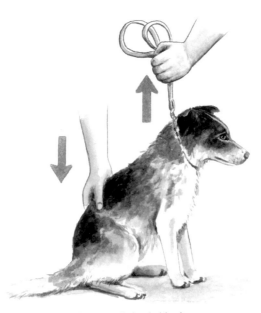

Push the puppy's backside down as you pull up on his head. At the same time say, "Sit" in a firm, confident voice.

correctly. Attach the training lead to the free end of the collar, making certain that the collar will move freely.

There are several approaches to teaching a dog to sit. Probably the easiest method is to position your dog on your left, take up the slack in your lead and say "*Fleet, sit.*" A moment later, push the dog's rear downward. Keep its head up with the leash to prevent its first *sit* attempts from becoming *downs.* Always say the dog's name, followed about a second later by the *sit* command. Your voice should be loud and firm enough to be heard, but yelling is not required.

The first attempts at getting a *sit* out of your border collie will probably not be all that elegant. If it is particularly shy, it may try to back up or fight the leash. Give it time to recover and get used to the idea that you are not going to strangle it or crush its pelvis.

If you have even the approximation of a *sit*, lavish the dog with praise. Do not get so carried away that you scare it, but let it know you approve.

If your dog resists the downward push on its rear, try putting pressure on the back of its "knees." If it sits or half-sits then, praise and pet it.

Allow your border collie to get back to its feet and start all over. Keeping its head up, say "*Fleet, sit,*" and push the dog's rear downward. You should expect the *sit* to be better and more complete this time. If it actually sits or comes closer to sitting, praise it again. With repetition and consistency, your border collie will begin to sit when it hears "*Sit.*"

Stay

Your border collie will have to have a good handle on the *sit* command before you can teach it to *stay.*

Start the training exercise by sitting your border collie next to your left leg. When it is settled, say "*Stay*" and move a step away from your dog. At the same time you take your step, put your hand in front of the dog's face. If your pet moves, put it back in position. Let it sit for a second or two, then say "*OK*" and allow it to come to you. If it has done well, praise it—make it clear that you are pleased with what it has done. In the early stages the young border collie will probably not understand why you are so pleased. It will understand only that you are pleased and will work to continue pleasing you.

As you repeat the training steps above, gradually increase the distance that you move from your border collie and the time it *stays*. The *stay* is as demanding of consistency as any of the commands in obedience training. You will have to watch the young dog closely after issuing the *stay* command. If it fidgets or leans, it will likely stand and you have to move quickly to keep it seated. Put your hand in front of its face and say "*Stay*" again. Eventually, you will be able to move well away from your dog and leave it sitting for a considerable time.

Remember that your dog is new to the *stay* command. A high-energy dog like the border collie does not naturally stay in one place for very long. Before it can learn to *stay*, it must successfully stay for a few seconds. Do not get impatient and punish your dog. That can only lead to confusion and the necessity of retraining. Keep things light and the sessions short, especially at the beginning.

Come

After your dog has learned to *sit* and *stay*, it is ready to master the *come* command. Your border collie has very likely been coming to you since it arrived, but now you need to teach it that "*Come*" is a command and not a whim.

Give your pet the *sit* command followed by the *stay* command. Walk to the end of the training lead and turn to

Young border collies may work well with older dogs but they do not learn from them.

face your dog. Put all the enthusiasm you can into your voice and say, "*Fleet, come*." If the dog does not come immediately, give a gentle tug on the training lead. If it still does not come, tug a little harder. When your dog comes to you, praise and pet it. Let it know that you are pleased.

After you have rewarded your border collie with praise, let it calm down for a few minutes. Give the *sit/stay* command again. Move to the end of the leash, face your dog, and say "*Fleet, come*" in an excited voice. Again, use the lead to encourage the dog to come if it is hesitant. Be extravagant with praise when your dog does what you want of it.

When you have your border collie coming dependably within the length of the training lead, place your pup on a longer lead. There are a number of commercially made leads for use in training. You can also make a perfectly good lead like the dragline described on page 60, Training for Stock Work section.

A border collie in proper heeling position will move in step with the handler, but will not be under foot.

No matter which lead you decide to use, the idea is to gradually increase the distance between you and your dog before the *come* command is given. When you have reached the end of the longer lead, usually about 20 feet (6.1 m), you can begin to work off lead.

No dog should ever be called to its handler to be punished. Even mild correction should not be given if the border collie has just obeyed a *come* command. Border collies are exceptionally bright. Not only can they learn to come quickly, they can learn *not* to come if something unpleasant is done to them after they obey. Nothing is more frustrating than calling a border collie and having it sit 8 or 10 yards (7–9 m) from you and watch while you call.

Come may be the most critical of the commands in the set discussed here. A dog that will come instantly on command is a convenience to the handler/trainer. More importantly, the lives of any number of rambunctious young border collies have been saved because they turned to go to their owners when called.

Heel

The *heel* command is one of the handiest commands you can teach your dog. It makes moving around in crowds with your dog easy, even pleasant. The idea of the *heel* command is to teach your border collie to stay on your left, starting and stopping when you do.

Begin by giving the *sit/stay* command. The dog should be positioned to your left as in the beginning stages of the *sit* command. Take up the slack in the lead, putting light upward pressure on the training collar. Hold the lead in your right hand as you step forward off your left foot. As you make your first step, say "*Rip, heel.*" If Rip does not step out with you, urge him forward with a gentle tug on the training collar. If he hesitates, get his attention by popping the loose end of the lead against your leg. Repeat the command, name and all, as you walk forward. If he moves with you, praise him. Keep moving with the pup's shoulders just even with your legs. If he moves ahead or lags behind, correct him with light pressure on his collar. If he gets completely out of line, stop what you are doing, give him the *sit/stay* command, and start over.

If Rip moves well with you, continue praising him as you walk. When you stop, give the *sit* command. Ultimately, he will learn that he should sit when you stop and walk at heel when you step off on the left foot.

Your pet should focus its attention on you as you walk. Getting the undivided attention of an energetic young border collie may take some work; the younger the border collie, the more work it will take.

Some handlers will make sudden changes in direction in order to keep their dog's attention on them. Others recommend that the trainer carry a piece of raw liver in his or her mouth while working the dog. Not surprisingly, the direction change method has met with greater popularity than the liver technique.

If you keep at it, your border collie will heel without a leash. Working off lead is especially handy if you have an arm full of packages. If you move around in crowded areas or plan to compete in obedience trials, the *heel* command is critical.

Teach the down command by gently pulling the border collie down from a sitting position. At the same time, say "Down" in a firm voice.

Down

The *down* command is particularly useful for border collies that will later be trained for stock work—in fact, the *down* command is a prerequisite for stock work. It is also vital for anyone who takes a border collie out around other people.

Start *down* training with your border collie to your left, just as you did when beginning *sit* training. The training collar should be on your dog correctly and the training lead attached. Give your dog the *sit/stay* command. Say to your dog, "*Sam, down.*" Use the lead to pull his head down.

Some border collies will be frightened at being pulled downward. If your dog shows signs of anxiety, stop what you are doing until it calms down. Give the *sit/stay* command again and use the chain to pull its head downward again. If any progress is made toward an elbow down, stomach on the ground position, praise and pet your dog. After praising the dog and allowing it time to calm down, return it to the sit/stay position. Repeat the *down* command using your dog's name. Again, pull downward on the training lead. If your dog moves toward the down position, lavish it with praise. If you take your time and remain patient, your border collie will lose its fear of being downed.

Some border collies are stubborn about being downed. Large males may be particularly difficult. With these animals you may have to take a different tack. Position your dog to your left and give the *sit/stay* command. Repeat "*Sam, down.*" Pull downward on the training lead. If he refuses to move downward, grasp both of his front legs just below the knee, gently fold his legs, and position him on the ground. Praise him extravagantly. Let him calm down for a few minutes before you start over. It will not take long for your border collie to learn that *down* means he should take a position with elbows and stomach on the ground. This method also works well with shy dogs.

Down/stay: After your dog has mastered the *down*, you can begin work on the *down/stay* combination. Training for this combination is identical to the *sit/stay* command combination, except the *down* precedes the *stay*.

The *down* command is especially helpful in controlling excitable young border collies. A border collie in the down position has to do more shifting and bunching in order to get out of a down position than a sit position. A perceptive trainer can catch a pup before it can break its down. With patience and time, a border collie can be downed and left for extended periods.

If the trainer has its trust, a border collie will do almost everything asked of him.

Training for Stock Work

Border collies have been bred for centuries to move livestock from one place to the other. It is in this arena that they truly shine. While all border collies have some degree of working potential, not all are excellent working prospects. Except in extreme cases, the only way to tell if a border collie will develop into a good stock dog is to start training it. During the training process, weaknesses such as timidity or oversensitivity may show themselves. Some flaws can be trained out of the border collie but it is impossible to train courage. If your border collie shows cowardice during training, it may not be cut out for stock work. On the other hand, cowardice, or what looks like cowardice, can be trained into the border collie. It is not uncommon that someone will start a normally bold young dog on adult cattle or bad-tempered rams. It will not take an intelligent puppy long to learn that cattle equal pain. After it makes that association, you will notice a certain lack of enthusiasm concerning livestock.

There is a common misconception that a female border collie will train her puppies in stock work. That just will not happen. The mother may snap at puppies that get in her way while she is working, but all she is doing is getting them out from underfoot. If you want a "finished" working border collie, you will have to do the finishing yourself or pay someone to do it for you.

Minimum Preparatory Training

Before you train your border collie to work stock, you will have to have some degree of control over it. At a minimum your border collie will need to be leash trained, trained to *down* on command, and to *come*. This training can start when the border collie is old enough to pay attention, between two and four months of age. Early training sessions should be limited to no longer than 15 minutes. If you have time during the day, you can schedule multiple 15-minute sessions. If you choose to push the training sessions much past 15 minutes, you run the risk of "souring" your border collie, a phenomenon that occurs commonly in the training of all animals, when

A border collie shows off a little at a demonstration.

the animal finds the training, or the activity for which it is being trained, unpleasant. If you push your border collie too hard, you may find that it does not want to work at all. Take your time, spread the work over several sessions per day, and give your puppy time to mature.

Basic Equipment for Stock Work

There are a few minimum pieces of equipment required for training a border collie on stock:

• One piece of equipment you may need is a long cane pole, such as those sold at a fishing supply store. Cut off the small end until you come to a piece that is fairly substantial. You will need to keep about 12 feet (3.7 m) of the pole. Pad the narrow end of the pole. Surgical gauze may be used for the padding. Tape the gauze with adhesive tape or the stretch tape frequently used to wrap horses' leg joints.

• Next, you will need a dragline. A dragline may be made from a 20-foot (6.1 m) piece of quarter-inch nylon rope. Bind a snap, swivel into one end, and tie a large knot in the other. You will find all the makings for the dragline at your local hardware store.

• Of course, you will also need stock—sheep, goats, or ducks will do to start young dogs. Cattle, particularly adult cattle, should be saved until the pup gets its feet under it.

• Finally, you will need an enclosed area to work your border collie. A small paddock or round pen will serve if it is clear of trees, brush, and tall grass.

Basic Training for Working Stock

Before your border collie will be of maximum benefit to you, it must be taught some minimum command sets. Along with the *down* command it should know at the beginning of its stock training, it must be taught to differentiate its right from its left. These commands are referred to as the *flanking* commands. Your border collie will

A young border collie demonstrates a right-hand flanking move on angora goats.

also need to know to approach stock, on command, to get around the stock, and how to put the stock in a pen.

The Flanking Commands

The easy way to "put flanking commands on" a border collie is to put the

Fetching, or bringing stock toward the handler, is natural for border collies.

Walk slowly away from the stock, allowing them to move toward you. In a firm voice say, "Walk up."

trainee in a pen with you and some stock. A border collie's natural instinct is to bring stock toward its handler. If you walk into an enclosed area with a young border collie, it will normally move around the stock in the enclosure until it is directly across the flock from you. If you move clockwise, the young border collie will move clockwise in order to stay directly across from you. If you move counterclockwise, you will find your border collie moving counterclockwise in an effort to stay in front of you.

As you move to your right, speak the command you want your border collie to associate with moving to the right. Traditionally, this command is, "*Way to Me*." The traditional command for the left flank is "*Come By*." These are the most commonly used commands for flanking, but there is no magic in them; use any command you like. Some trainers use "*right*" and "*left*"; others have used the Spanish words for right and left (*derecha* and *izquierda*). Some will never use voice commands at all. They substitute whistle commands entirely. What matters is that you settle on commands for left and right and stick to them.

The appropriate flanking command should be given just before you move. If everything works as it should, the trainee will move in opposition to you. When you stop, give your border collie its *down* command. Wait a few seconds before you move again. Issue the correct command just before you move. If your border collie does not move as anticipated, use the padded pole to nudge it in the right direction. You are not punishing the pup, just encouraging it. Try to remember that there is a difference between encouragement and hitting for distance. One or two good bashes with the cane and your pup will muster out of stock work on its own.

Practice the flanks until your border collie gets the hang of it. When it moves upon command, in the direction you have requested, you have successfully "put its flanks on it." Later, you will use the flanking commands to teach more advanced work.

If your border collie does not want to stop when it is started, break out the dragline. Issue your pup's *down* command in a loud voice. If your dog continues to move or chases the stock, repeat the command and step on the dragline. The pup will literally hit the end of its rope a couple of times, then make the association between not going down on command and the sudden stop. Most dogs do not enjoy the sensation of being jerked off their feet. In short order, most border collies will *down* immediately.

The Fetch

By nature, border collies are "fetching" dogs—they will do everything they can to bring the stock *toward* the handler. Most other breeds of stockdogs are "driving dogs"—they are genetically engineered to push stock *away* from their handler. In teaching your dog to fetch, you will be using its inbred instincts to aid you.

Use the flanking commands to position your border collie directly across the flock from you. Down the pup and back away from the livestock. Typically, ducks or sheep will move away from the dog and toward you. As soon as the stock moves, call the dog in. It should ease into the stock very gradually. This gathering of the stock is referred to as the "lift." The traditional command to get a border collie to move into the stock is "*Walk Up.*" If the trainee is slow to rise, use the clicking or smacking sounds most people use to encourage their dogs. If your dog still does not move, use the dragline to get it to its feet and moving toward the stock. After the stock has moved a good distance, down your border collie and realign it with the stock. Move back slowly, allowing the stock to move toward you. Again, call the puppy in on the stock and allow it to move them. Repeat the steps above until your dog will "come onto" the stock without hesitation.

Never let the pup rush the stock. If it becomes excited and charges the stock, jerk the pup up short with the dragline or use the pole to keep it at a distance. If your border collie persists in charging the flock, take it back to basic training. Be sure you can down it on command. Do not write the pup off if it is excitable. Training, practice, and hard work can put your border collie under control.

The Outrun

The outrun is the part of stock work in which the border collie runs out around the stock. Ideally, a perfect outrun at distance will be pear-shaped. The border collie should leave the handler's side and travel at something of an angle. As it nears the stock, the dog should swing wide until it is directly across from the handler. At that point the border collie should down or stop. A well-executed circular outrun is acceptable, but the pear-

Use a fenced lane to teach your border collie to drive. The fences will keep the stock from scattering and help keep the pup from circling them.

shaped outrun is more efficient and less tiring for the dog.

Under no circumstances should the dog change sides as it runs out to the stock. If it is sent to the right, it should stay on the right side. A "crossover" is considered a serious problem in trials and applied ranch work. The outrun should be wide enough that the stock is not disturbed as the border collie goes around them.

Except for penning, the outrun will require more work than any other training in the basic group. To start, outrun training is very much like training for flanks. The primary difference is that the dog will start each exercise at the handler's side. Position your border collie as you want it and down it. Using a loud, excited voice, issue the flanking command to send your dog in the direction you want it to go. It will help the dog get wide of the stock if you

A good shed requires the border collie to turn one or more sheep away from the flock. The handler can make a break in the flock but is not allowed to turn stock.

position it on the side of you that is opposite the direction you want it to go. If it is to be sent right, position it to your left and force it to run wide around you.

If your border collie cuts in close to the stock, force it out by running alongside it. This is another place where the long pole may be used to force the young dog even wider.

As the pup gets the knack of the outrun, increase the distance from the starting point to the stock a little at a time. Be certain that the dog is positioned correctly before giving it the flanking command that will start the outrun. If your dog does something incorrect, stop and correct it. A loud, shouted, "*No!*", will serve to let it know that it has erred. Never let your trainee get by with anything. Eventually, you should have your border collie making outruns of 250 to 400 yards (229–366 m).

Advanced Training for Working Stock

Advanced training involves two aspects that go against the border collie's inherited behavioral tendencies. The *drive* and the *shed* are the most difficult things to teach a border collie.

The drive: *Driving*, the act of pushing stock away from the handler, is entirely contrary to border collies'

genetic heritage. For countless generations they have been bred to fetch livestock toward their handlers. A border collie puppy that is placed in a pen with lambs, ducks, or even kittens will make every effort to move to the side of the stock opposite its owner. Typically, the animals will move away from the pup; as a result, they will move toward the handler.

The easiest way to train a border collie to the *drive* is to find a lane that is fenced on both sides. Move your stock into the lane and place your border collie in the lane between you and the stock. Give the dog the command to *walk up* on the stock. Some dogs will *walk up* with no hesitation and begin the drive. Most, however, will make every effort to get around the stock to begin the *fetch*. The purpose of the fenced lane is to help keep the stock moving in a straight line and to discourage the border collie from running around the stock.

The pup may be confused about this change in direction. You will have to be very patient with the young border collie at this point. If it tries to move around the stock, *down* it and let the stock move a little ahead of it. Again, give the command to *walk up*. The stock should begin to move away from the dog. If it moves too far to the right or left, use the flanking command to center it on the stock, and allow it to continue. If it becomes confused or presses too hard, down it and allow the stock to move ahead a little. Give the command to *walk up* again. The idea is to get the young dog used to the act of staying between the handler and the stock. It will take time and patience.

If you do not happen to have a fenced lane, put the stock against a fence and *down* the dog behind them. Since you will not have two fences to work against, you will have to help the dog hold the stock against the fence. There is also the problem of the dog going around the stock. You will have to be more cautious with the border collie when you have only one fence available and be sure that you do not let the stock bolt or let the border collie get around the stock.

The shed: The *shed* is another extremely difficult and useful exercise for border collies. If you have ever seen a cutting horse work, you have a concept of the *shed*. In the *shed*, the handler will string the stock out in a line. The border collie will be positioned directly across the flock from the handler who will use the dog and himself or herself to move the stock between himself or herself and the dog. As the stock strings through, the handler will force a break and call the border collie in. It is the border collie's job at this point to hold the animal the handler has singled out away from the rest of the flock. The border collie's natural instinct is to keep stock together in a group. Training a young dog to split a flock takes some work.

Once the handler makes the break in the string of stock and calls the border collie in, he or she must get the dog to face in the right direction. All the animal's instincts and training are to gather the flock, to put the stray back in with the larger group. You may have to walk toward the animal you have singled out and call the border collie to you. Your border collie may hesitate, trying to decide what to do. If it is faced in the right direction shout "*This one*," and tell it to "*walk up*." Use "*This one*" or some other command every time you call your dog in for the *shed*. In time, you can

The energy, focus, and athleticism of the breed is obvious in this border collie.

dispense with calling it in or telling it to *walk up*.

If your dog hesitates when you call it in, encourage it by smacking your lips, stomping your feet, or clucking. Anything you can do to get it moving toward the animal will help. If it still hesitates, move quickly so that the animal to be *shed* is between you and the dog. Its border collie instincts to *fetch* the stock to the handler should kick in. Once your dog picks up on the idea of *shedding*, stop moving behind the stock. That approach is only for early training.

While handlers have to create a gap in the line of stock, they should never turn the animals; the border collie must do that.

Nutrition

Dietary Requirements

Feeding your border collie is a combination of tightrope walking and consistency. All dogs have minimum and maximum requirements for their dietary needs. Protein, fats, and carbohydrates make up the bulk of dog foods and must be present in the correct proportions. Minerals such as calcium and phosphorous are also necessary as are the multitude of vitamins that cause such confusion in human diets. If your border collie does not get the correct amounts of all the nutritional components, it will be something less than it could be. In extreme instances, diets that lacked vital nutritional elements have resulted in border collies that were deficient mentally.

Protein

When most people think of dietary requirements for dogs, they think of protein. While it is true that wild canids and feral dogs are carnivores, their diets also include things other than just meat. Feral and wild canids do kill and eat other animals, but they eat all of the animals they kill. If you have ever chanced upon a fresh dog or coyote kill, you may have noticed that the first things eaten in such kills are the intestines and their contents. By eating the contents of the intestines, the canids get a rich supply of vegetable matter and some enzymes that they cannot produce themselves. The point here is that dogs in their natural state do not eat an all-meat diet; it is liberally supplemented with vegetable matter.

Commercial dog food manufacturers include protein from a variety of sources including soybean meal, horse meat, beef, chicken, fish meal, and various combinations of "processed" parts and leftovers. Of course, meat- and fish-based protein sources are digested more easily than plant-based sources. Kibble most commonly uses grain and soybean sources, semimoist foods are typically soybean based, while canned foods are entirely meat or meat and grain combinations.

All dogs—border collies are no exception—require protein for growth, normal body maintenance, hair production, and as building blocks for healing after injuries. Puppies and pregnant bitches require higher levels of protein than adult and older dogs.

There is great controversy about how much protein is required, the protein source(s), and how protein should be distributed over a border collie's life.

Carbohydrates

Carbohydrates are a source of energy in dog foods. Typically, carbohydrates in dog foods are derived from grain sources such as wheat or corn. The energy from carbohydrates is not as readily available to your dog as the energy from fats since it requires a more complex digestive process. It is from carbohydrates and fats that your border collie will derive all of its energy at the cellular level.

Fats

Dogs need, and can use, much more fat in their diets than humans. High-fat foods are generally more appealing to dogs than low-fat products. Humans, too, find the taste of fat and fat-based foods more appealing than their low- or no-fat equivalents. (If you doubt this, compare the taste of a regular potato chip against the taste of a baked chip.)

Your border collie will need minimum amounts of fat to maintain a healthy coat, a normally functioning neural system, and as a delivery medium for fat-soluble vitamins.

The downside to this is that fats, while easily converted into energy in active dogs, are just as easily converted into body fats in less active pets. You and your veterinarian need to monitor the body fat of your border collie and either adjust its activity level or its fat intake.

Vitamins

Most premium dog foods contain all of the minimum daily requirement of vitamins for your border collie, but in rare instances some supplements may be required. Vitamins, in the correct amounts and proportions, are absolutely necessary. When the amounts are not correct or the proportions are not in balance, your border collie may be harmed. Growing puppies are particularly subject to problems related to vitamin overdose. Discuss this with your veterinarian.

Minerals

Minerals are another dietary essential that can be overdone. Calcium, necessary for bone, teeth, and muscle development, has been linked to osteochondritis desicans (OCD) in puppies (see OCD, page 74). Generally, all minerals required by your border collie will be present in a good-quality food. Find a food that meets your dog's needs and stick with it. Or, use a food recommended by your breeder or veterinarian.

The Effects of Good Early Nutrition

Puppy nutrition begins with feeding practices. Puppies should be fed from a bowl that can be cleaned easily. If they are to be fed in the house, they should be fed in a quiet, out of the way area. They should be fed four times daily at the same time for each meal. When they reach three months, feedings should be cut back to three times daily, then to twice daily. At one year of age, puppies may be fed once daily. If there is more than one puppy to be fed, they should be fed separately in order to better monitor each pup's food intake. More importantly, separate feeding prevents stronger pups from getting all the food and the smaller ones from starving.

Your border collie puppy will continue to grow until it is 18 months to two years old. Since the pup will be as tall as it ever will be at age nine months to one year, there is a tendency to assume it is full grown. While that assumption does no real damage, feeding an immature dog as if it were an adult can.

Except for pregnant bitches, puppies need more protein than other dogs. A premium-quality puppy food will generally provide sufficient protein. Even puppies that grow as fast as border collies can get what they need from commercial foods. Recently, there has been some dispute as to how long immature border collies should be kept on puppy food. Manufacturers recommend that growing dogs be kept on puppy food for a full year. In contrast, some canine nutritionists feel that puppies should be changed to adult dog food at age three months. The first recommendation may be based on the belief that when dogs eat puppy food for 12 months, the dog food company will sell more puppy food. The second recommendation is based on a belief that too much protein in a puppy's diet can result in such problems as osteochondritis desicans. A diet too low in protein can produce an adult border collie

A calm, confident border collie will accept any situation, even being posed in a studio.

are supposed to be tuck-waisted. A border collie in excellent physical condition will invariably appear skinny, at least when it is wet. If your border collie is passing a veterinarian's examination, has normal energy for a border collie, and does eat, do not worry about playing musical dog foods.

Border collies operate at full throttle for most of their waking time. As a result, they generally require a higher-energy food than most other breeds. Energy is provided in most dog foods in the form of fat. The more fat in a dog food, the more potential energy is available to the dog.

Labels

The proportions of fat and protein contained in a dog food are typically printed boldly on the label or the outside of the bag. At the very least, a federally required label will provide the nutritional breakdown of the product it represents. Fat percentages in most dog foods will range from 8 percent to 15 percent, rarely higher. Most active border collies can make it on a feed with 12 percent fat. If your dog begins to lose weight or just runs out of juice during a normal work day, you have two options. You either need to up its ration of feed or change to a feed with a higher percentage fat.

Changing the Diet

If you decide that your best option is to change feed, do it over a period of a month or so. Start the change by feeding a mixture of 10 percent new feed, 90 percent old feed. By the end of the first week, have the percentage 25/75. Gradually increase the new food in the mix until you are feeding 100 percent of the new food. If your border collie shows signs of stomach distress or a runny stool, move back to a higher percentage of the old food. If you find that your dog cannot tolerate the new food at any percentage, aban-

that is less than it could have been, both physically and mentally.

What Is Different about Border Collie Nutrition?

There are two big differences between border collies and some collective prototype of all other dogs in the matter of nutrition. The first difference is that border collies are not normally big eaters. After the glutton stage that all dogs go through as puppies, they will tend to be thrifty eaters. Even the rare border collie that does eat large amounts of food, will tend to eat a little here, a little there. First-time border collie owners may be tempted to add treats to their dog's diet or even change foods. Unless there is some other reason to think that your border collie is not getting enough to eat, do not bother. Remember, border collies

don it. Wait a couple of weeks until the dog stabilizes; then find a new food and start the gradual change again.

If, on the other hand, your border collie begins to gain weight, cut back on its ration or switch to a feed with a lower overall percentage of fat. Some manufacturers provide premium dog foods that differ only in the proportions of fat and protein.

Commercial Diets— Pros and Cons

In the dog food section of your local supermarket you can find dry dog food, canned dog food, semisoft dog food, and even frozen dog food. There are gourmet foods, hypoallergenic foods, all-beef foods, all-chicken foods, all-turkey foods, and foods with mixtures of meats and vegetables. You will also find multicolored kibble, kibble in interesting shapes, and kibble with shapes that do not have any real reason for existence. Some commercial semisoft food looks like chunks of raw meat, some of the canned food looks like your Aunt Martha's beef stew and some canned dog food looks as if the dog has already eaten it once.

Before you get too tangled up in the dog food marketing dilemma, there are several things you should remember: First, dogs are red/green color-blind; dog food could well be fuschia and the dog would not know. Second, your border collie has probably never been to dinner at your Aunt Martha's and has no idea what her beef stew looks like. Finally, few dogs are horticulturists—they cannot distinguish a pea from a carrot, or from anything else, for that matter. They do not care about their food's appearance. The dog food's aroma and taste—aroma being the most important—are the critical factors to your dog. Be forewarned that what smells awful to you may smell wonderful to your dog. Some perfectly

With a normal canine sense of smell and the border collie's intelligence, the breed has excelled at tracking.

acceptable canned dog foods may actually cause you to gag when you open them, but, if you can stand the odor and your border collie does well on the food, use the food.

There is constant controversy today about the contents of dog foods, particularly canned dog foods. If you browse through pet journals or the Internet you will find printed or electronic sermons on every aspect of canine nutrition. Some of the pitches will be about "natural" diets for dogs, others will be excited about what goes into dog food, others will rattle on and on about all meat diets. Some of these diatribes contain completely valid information and there is the catch—this core of truth can steer you away from perfectly good sources of canine nutrition.

The truth is, most premium commercial dog foods are more than adequate for your border collie's nutritional needs. You may have to pick and choose, but what your dog needs is already readily available. Working with your veterinarian, you should be able to find a premium-quality food that will fit your pet's needs.

Kibble versus Canned Foods

The most commonly used forms of dog food are kibble and canned foods, in that order. Both have characteristics to recommend them. There are also things about kibbled and canned foods that argue against their use.

Kibbled foods, for our purposes, will be defined as a dog food made up primarily of vegetable products with added fat. Kibbled foods may also have added fish or animal protein sources. Typically, kibble is sold in bags, although some kibble is sold in small boxes. Kibble is the food of choice for individuals with a large number of dogs. It is relatively less expensive than other types of dog food of similar quality. The most expensive kibble is still less expensive than canned foods offering the same ingredients and quality.

Because kibble is dry it is also easier to feed, less messy, and generally more pleasant to be around than most canned

Dog foods come in an amazing array of flavors, types, and contents.

foods. Kibbled foods are also more easily measured when monitoring food intake. Some kibble is as nutritious as any other form of dog food, but there is a catch. No matter the nutritional value of a dog food, if it is not eaten it does no good.

Some dogs absolutely will not eat kibble. A great deal of what a dog will eat is determined by their early diets and how much they can manipulate you. If you have a picky dog and feel compelled to feed kibble for financial or other reasons, you may be able to strike a happy medium. Select a premium-quality kibble; if the dog will not eat the kibble, top-dress it with a little canned food. The canned food will provide a more appealing taste for your border collie, the kibble will provide texture—something for the dog to chew—and the combination will keep the cost reasonable.

Canned food is easily stored and all it takes to prepare it is a can opener, a feed bowl of some sort, and a dog that is agreeable to being fed. The single most important recommendation for canned food is that dogs find it more appealing than other forms of food.

The downside to canned food is that it is considerably more expensive than kibbled foods. The cost of feeding canned food can be prohibitive, especially if more than one dog is involved.

No need to go overboard with the canned food. A quarter of a can should be more than enough to tempt your border collie's taste buds.

Roll-Your-Own Dog Rations

There is a tendency in all of us to want to believe that by adding this or that we can make a perfect dog food. A few generations ago anyone offering a commercial dog food would have been bankrupt shortly after beginning production. People fed dogs what they had left over from the table. Families were larger then; people ate more and had more leftovers. True, puppy mortality was probably higher, more dogs very likely suffered from problems that could have been handled by a better diet, and a lot of dogs never reached their true potential.

In recent years, dog-feeding practices have been greatly changed by a general decline in family size. There has also been a shift of population from rural areas to cities and suburbs. The ready availability of relatively inexpensive commercial dog foods has had its impact on dog feeding. The vast majority of dog owners feed a premium kibbled or canned food. Certainly, the vast majority of professional breeders and trainers feed only a commercially prepared product appropriate to the breed, the activity of the dog, and its age. It is an excellent example to follow.

The single biggest problem with home cooking your dog food is getting everything in balance. Too much protein in a young dog's diet could lead to OCD as can too much calcium. Too much fat in the home-brewed feed can create overweight pets. It is especially difficult to get the right balance of vitamins and minerals. An unbalanced diet can cause growth difficulties, orthopedic problems, and other physical and mental problems too great to list.

If you are pondering going into the dog food business at home, answer the following questions:

1. How is your border collie doing on its present diet?
2. Have you spoken to your veterinarian about your pet's diet?
3. Do you know what should be included in a dog food?
4. Do you know where to get the ingredients you will need?
5. Do you have the facilities you will need for making your creation?
6. Can you afford the homemade dog food?
7. Do you have a complete organic chemistry lab in your basement?
8. Do you have the time to put into making the food?
9. Can you actually make something better for your border collie than a commercial manufacturer, especially considering the varieties of food on the market?

If the answer to question number one is "OK," or "Great," then why bother making your own food. If the answer to question two is, "No," you are definitely getting ahead of yourself. If the answers to questions three through nine are "No," dig deeper into the available commercially produced dog foods for something that will suit your requirements and your pet's needs.

As with any other canine health-related question, you should consult your veterinarian before you do anything drastic. If you find that your veterinarian will not provide the information you need, consider another veterinarian. If you cannot get information you need locally, try your state school of veterinary medicine.

Dietary Requirements in Old Age

As dogs age they tend to become less active than when they were pups. Old age in border collies may not arrive until age 12 or more. As they slow they may gain weight if their nutritional intake is not adjusted. Neutered dogs and older dogs may share this characteristic. Fats should certainly be reduced in the older border collie's diet; without the youthful activity, a high-fat diet can result in a high-fat border collie. The fats removed from the older dog's diet should be replaced with carbohydrates.

Commercial manufacturers produce a variety of products for older dogs. Depending upon your border collie's activity level, history of injuries, and age, you should be able to find a food suitable to its needs. Consult with your veterinarian before making drastic changes.

The intensity of its gaze and the thickness of its coat are testimony to the quality of this border collie's diet.

Your Border Collie's Health

History of the Health of Border Collies

Because border collies are working stock, they have developed the reputation of being disease-free. They are hardy by nature and tend to recover more rapidly than most dogs from cuts, breaks, and other trauma, but border collies have medical problems just like any other breed. Most probably stories about their genetic perfection arose about the time of their first introduction into America. Farmers along the English and Scottish border were not prone to "carry" a dog that could not pull its own weight, and any border collie displaying a physical disability was disposed of. As a result, very few border collies of the time were genetically flawed.

As the modern border collie developed, inbreeding occurred as a necessity. Wiston Cap, the 1965 International Champion, had Richardson's Cap in his pedigree 17 times. Because of the quality of his work and his intelligence, Wiston Cap was a popular sire. There are very few modern border collies that do not have Wiston Cap somewhere in their pedigree. From this, it is easy to see how the presence of genetic flaws might have spread in the breed.

The Most Common Health Problems in Border Collies

Border collies have the same problems with contagious diseases as other breeds and are bothered by their share of genetic diseases. The most common noncontagious health problems in the breed are: hip dysplasia, progressive retinal atrophy (PRA), collie eye, and osteochondritis desicans (OD).

Hip Dysplasia

Hip dysplasia is a failure of the ball socket in the hip to develop as it should.

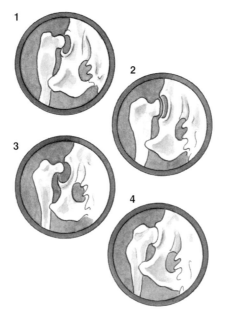

Hip dysplasia:
1. Acetabulum (socket) is shallow, some subluxation (partial dislocation) is present
2. Head of femur is flattened, luxation (dislocation) is evident
3. A milder case of hip dysplasia with partial subluxation (partial dislocation)
4. A normal hip with no evidence of damage to the femur of any obvious subluxation.

Cartilage and natural fluids make a smooth, well-cushioned joint within the socket. In a normal dog, the ball joint of the leg is fully encased by the socket of the hip, but in a dysplastic dog the socket does not cover the ball joint completely. Cartilage and other lubricants may also be absent. In extreme cases, the ball joint is held against the pelvis only through the tension of the dog's leg and hip muscles.

Although hip dysplasia has been associated with such environmental factors as diet and exercise, the best documented cause of canine hip dysplasia (CHD) is genetics. CHD is polygenic; the genes involved are numerous. Because of the complexity of the gene interactions in CHD, there may be varying degrees of severity in puppies from the same litter. Some may evidence no dysplasia while others may be so severely crippled that they must be euthanized.

Signs: Puppies may show signs of hip dysplasia as early as two weeks of age. As the puppy grows, it may not be as active as a normal puppy. There may also be a reluctance to climb onto and off raised surfaces. The owner may also notice a dysplastic pup sitting with its pelvis cocked noticeably to one side. Some dogs may also "wobble" while walking, especially if tired. Owners should also be concerned if the chest and front legs of the animal are obviously much better developed than the hips. In extreme cases, the affected dog may yelp or whine when required to move.

OFA certification: While all of the behaviors listed above should be cause for concern, only a complete orthopedic and radiographic examination can accurately diagnose hip dysplasia. The Orthopedic Foundation for Animals (OFA) certifies hips and other joints as severe, moderate, fair, good, and excellent. OFA only issues these certifications for animals two years old

and older. It is especially important when selecting a puppy that both of its parents be certified by OFA.

Treatment: In moderate cases of hip dysplasia, treatment may be as simple as administering a couple of aspirin a day. Some dysplastic dogs may benefit from surgery. Triple pelvic osteotomy is a type of surgery in which the pelvis is cut and repositioned to force a better fit between the femur and hip socket. More extreme cases may require complete hip replacement. Since hip surgery is expensive, it may not be an option for all dysplastic dogs. Consult your veterinarian before you undertake any treatment. In a small portion of diagnosed hip dysplasia cases, the border collie must be euthanized.

Prevention: The only effective method of preventing hip dysplasia is simply not breeding border collies that carry the complex genes for the disorder. All dogs found to be dysplastic should be neutered immediately. No matter how much your dog means to you, breeding gene-defective animals does not improve the breed. There are many excellent border collies available, most of them without defective genes. Again, buy and breed only OFA-certified stock.

Osteochondritis Desicans (OCD)

OCD is a defect or damage to the cartilage overlying the bones in a joint. Bone damage may also be present, to the extent that slivers of bone may show up in X-rays. Signs of lameness may appear in puppies around four months of age, gradually increasing in severity until the animal is severely limited in its movements at twelve months old.

Causes: Suggested causes of the problem include greater than normal activity, leaping off couches or steps, a genetic predisposition to cartilage damage, and a diet too rich in protein and other nutrients.

Treatment: Treatment may be as simple as confining the puppy to limit movement or as extreme as surgery to remove damaged cartilage. Some veterinarians have had success combining confinement with a diet limited in protein.

Prevention: How do owners avoid OCD in their border collies? Suggestions include limiting activity until the pup is a year or more in age and feeding a puppy food that contains reasonable levels of protein, fat, and other nutrients. A discussion of puppy nutrition with your veterinarian could help decide the specific brand of puppy food you select. As to limiting the activity of a border collie puppy—good luck!

Progressive Retinal Atrophy

Progressive retinal atrophy (PRA) is just what the name implies: Dogs with PRA gradually lose visual receptors in the retina, ultimately resulting in blindness. Beginning at about two years of age, night blindness will occur, and by the age of five most PRA victims are completely blind. *All* border collies with PRA eventually go blind.

PRA can be detected in young dogs through the use of electroretinography. Since a complex cluster of genes controls PRA, it is difficult to predict the probability of a puppy having the disease. All border collies should be examined by a veterinary ophthalmologist. Many registries, breed clubs, and trial organizations provide low-cost or free examinations. It is not difficult to find an inexpensive way of having your animal tested. If you are considering a pup, ask to see its certificate. If a breeder cannot or will not provide PRA information, remember that many others will.

Collie Eye Anomaly (CEA)

Border collies along with standard collies, bearded collies, and Shetland sheepdogs, share the collie eye anomaly. It is the most common source of genetic blindness in the border collie. In recent years it has increased in frequency along with the increased popularity of the breed. As with PRA, all border collie puppies should be tested for CEA. If you are considering a puppy, make sure that all puppies in the litter are certified as normal. Because the genetic dynamics of CEA are so complex, it is easier to avoid it than control it. Again, good border collies are being bred every day; if you cannot find a completely CEA-free litter, look a little harder.

Seizures

Seizures result from the prolonged firing of the neurons in the brain. Causes include injury to the brain, response to toxic substances, and heredity. Sometimes there is no obvious cause. These cases are referred to as "idiopathic," which, in this instance, means, "I don't know where it comes from." In border collies the severity of the problem may vary greatly. Some border collies may simply appear to freeze in place or to ignore their owners briefly. Others may stagger and shake slightly. The most severe instances involve classic *grand mal* seizures in which the animal will fall to the ground and go into convulsions. Frequently, the dog may lose bladder and/or bowel control, may foam at the mouth, and, rarely, chew its own tongue.

If your border collie has seizures, perhaps the greatest danger arises from where the seizures occur. A border collie having seizures in the middle of a road is obviously in more danger than a border collie that has seizures in the kennel. Even *petit mal* seizures may cause your pet to fall off the top of its doghouse or down the steps. Border collies that live around water and are prone to seizures risk

Cold weather and the outdoors are a border collie's natural element.

All chemical treatments could have toxic side effects to the point of damage to the liver or kidneys. Your veterinarian or a competent veterinary neurologist will typically be glad to talk to you about potential problems with drug treatment. Of course, when the seizures are brought on by toxic substances or allergens, the logical approach is to remove the problem substance from the dog's environment.

Prevention: Ask the breeder of any dog you are considering if there are seizures in the bloodline. If the breeder will not talk to you about the history of seizures, there are other breeders.

Contagious Diseases

Following is a discussion of various contagious diseases for which vaccinations are available.

Rabies

Rabies is the most widely known disease of dogs. Of course, rabies does not discriminate and will attack all mammals. It is typically transmitted to healthy animals through the bite of an infected animal. There is some reason to believe that the virus that causes rabies can also be transmitted through the mucous membranes or through breaks in the skin.

After infection, there is an incubation period of from three weeks to 120 days; the average incubation time is four to six weeks. Two days after the end of the incubation period, the infected animal will either go into the "furious" or "dumb" state. The "furious" state is the excited state most associated with rabies. While in this stage, the animal becomes irritable and snaps at anything it encounters, thereby transmitting the disease again. During this stage the animal will begin to have difficulty swallowing. Large amounts of saliva accumulate in the mouth. Since the animal cannot swallow, the saliva flows out of the

falling into the water and drowning before they recover.

Usually, even severe seizures have little effect on the dog. Shortly after falling to the ground and convulsing, the victim of the seizures may be back on its feet, ready to play or work. However, when seizures come in series, or do not end quickly, there may be damage to the dog.

Treatment: Treatment for border collies with epilepsy (seizure disorder) is similar to the treatment for humans. Chemical treatments include Primadone, phenobarbital, Valium, Dilantin, and others. Potassium bromide or sodium bromide, used in conjunction with phenobarbital or Primadone, has proven highly effective in reducing seizures, but potassium bromide and sodium bromide are not commercially available to veterinarians. Both bromides must be bought as reagent grade chemicals and mixed with water by the veterinarian. There are other problems with using bromide treatments including relatively high toxicity. As of this writing, neither potassium bromide nor sodium bromide was on the Food and Drug Administration's (FDA) list of drugs approved for use with canine seizures.

mouth causing the characteristic "foaming at the mouth" characteristic of rabies. Though the rabid dog may be thirsty, it cannot drink. The dog may gag or cough, sometimes giving the impression that it has something stuck in its throat. Humans may be exposed to the virus at this point while trying to remove this nonexistent object. Within three to five days the infected animal will die of heart or respiratory failure.

"Dumb" rabies is simply rabies in which the excited stage is brief or skipped entirely. The animal dies just as surely and rapidly without the stereotypical behavior expected of rabid animals.

Prevention: Fortunately, rabies is easily avoided by inoculating pups between the ages of three and five months and administering annual inoculations. Most states require rabies inoculations by law and provide low-cost inoculations at convenient sites. If you are not sold on rabies inoculations, remember that it is almost always fatal when contracted. Even worse, the only method of verifying exposure to rabies is by removing the brain from the skull and examining it. Discuss the vaccinations with your veterinarian.

Distemper

Aside from rabies, distemper has always been the disease most feared by dog owners. Like rabies, distemper is caused by a virus. Although it can occur in older dogs, distemper occurs most frequently in young dogs between the age of two months and one year. It typically begins with cold-like symptoms such as a runny nose, elevated fever, sneezing, watery eyes, and general lassitude. If the dog does not recover, the disease may progress to diarrhea, convulsions, neural damage, and paralysis. Even if the dog survives this stage, it is likely to have chorea, an uncontrollable twitching of

Even the most withdrawn border collie has an expressive face.

the muscles. As distemper runs its course, the animal gradually becomes weaker and thinner. Death is common at this point.

If your border collie develops distemper or shows distemperlike symptoms, get it to the veterinarian as quickly as possible. Offer it as much liquid as it will drink and provide easily digested foods such as broth, egg yolks, and milk.

Prevention: Distemper is incurable, but it is preventable. Puppies should be vaccinated at eight weeks, at twelve weeks, and again at sixteen weeks. All dogs should receive annual boosters for distemper.

Like most of the diseases that afflict dogs, distemper is worse in underfed, or worm-infested, run-down dogs. After vaccination, keeping your border collie in good physical condition is the best method for preventing distemper.

Canine Parvovirus

When canine parvovirus (CPV) swept the United States in the late 1970s, whole kennels were devastated. Kennel owners would regularly lose every puppy, and sometimes, every dog in the kennel. Many border collie owners simply stayed home to avoid contact with the disease. There were stories of puppies that were healthy at breakfast and dead by dinner. Stories were rampant as to the source of the disease. One story held that CPV was a mutated feline distemper; other stories put forth the idea that canine distemper had somehow become more severe.

In truth, parvoviruses are present in most mammals. They have been proven to cause fatal illnesses in cattle, pigs, and a number of other animals. In humans, parvoviruses cause problems ranging from childhood rashes, to eye and upper respiratory inflammation, and spontaneous abortions in women.

Parvo is frequently fatal in dogs, puppies especially. It affects the intestinal tract, the heart, or both. When Parvo attacks the intestines, symptoms include general lassitude, extreme pain, loss of appetite, and vomiting. Shortly the dog's fever will spike and massive diarrhea will set in. Dogs, especially puppies, suffer dehydration and weaken.

Symptoms: Symptoms of Parvo's cardiac syndrome are most common in puppies. There is a loss of appetite, loud crying, and difficulty breathing. In this version of CPV, death may be sudden, but in some cases the animal lingers for days. Even when puppies survive the cardiac version of CPV, they may die months later from congestive heart failure.

Treatment: Treatment of CPV is difficult. It requires hospitalization, IV drips, and massive doses of antibiotics.

Prevention: As with distemper, the best treatment for CPV is prevention. Puppies should be kept away from public areas where infected dogs may have defecated. Inoculation is also important in preventing CPV. Most seven-in-one inoculations given by veterinarians include vaccines for Parvo. Following the standard vaccination schedule for puppies, adult dogs should get annual boosters for CPV. In areas where Parvo is a problem, semiannual boosters are recommended.

Coronavirus

Coronavirus is a parvovirus-like disease. While seldom fatal, coronavirus can debilitate a dog to the point that it may die of other diseases. Symptoms of this disease include bloody diarrhea with a foul odor. Coronavirus is more easily prevented than cured. Vaccines are available for coronavirus alone or in combination with other vaccines. A single dose is given, followed by a second dose two to three weeks later. In situations where puppies must be vaccinated prior to 12 weeks of age, an additional dose should be administered between 3 and 4 months of age. All dogs should be revaccinated annually.

Parainfluenza

The common problem of kennel cough is frequently associated with the parainfluenza virus, although any number of other infections are known by the same name. The virus causes a condition known as tracheobronchitis. The classic symptoms of this infection are a constant hacking cough combined with a loud, abrasive retching. The parainfluenza virus may be spread by contact with infected animals or by living in an infected kennel. It can also be communicated through the water droplets coughed up by infected dogs and transported by the wind.

Fortunately, the infection caused by the parainfluenza virus is usually not a serious problem but run-down or sickly animals may become even more sickly if parainfluenza is not treated quickly. Likewise, otherwise healthy border collies may weaken if parainfluenza is allowed to linger.

Prevention: The parainfluenza vaccine is included in the combination inoculations given to pups so make sure your border collie has had the entire series of inoculations as a pup. Annual boosters are necessary if the kennel cough and potential health problems associated with this virus are to be controlled.

Bordetella

Bordetella is a relatively mild bacterial infection that is frequently associated with tracheobronchitis. Its presence frequently complicates treatment of parainfluenza. It is easily controlled through vaccination so make sure your border collie is vaccinated against this opportunistic disease.

Borelliosis

Borelliosis, better known as Lyme disease, is an infection that can prove fatal in both dogs and humans. It is transmitted through the bite of the common deer tick. It has also been reported that crushing an infected tick against the skin can result in infection. Borelliosis is found in 48 of the 50 states but is most common in coastal states. Infected dogs run a high fever, lose their appetite, and develop acute joint pain. A variety of other symptoms have also been attributed to Lyme disease, including enlarged lymph nodes and eye problems, as well as kidney and heart disease.

Diagnosing and treating Lyme disease is difficult. There is a simple blood test that tests for serum antibodies against Borelliosis, but unfortunately, the uninfected dogs can test positive at a much higher rate than most veterinarians would like. The best diagnostic signs are the fever and joint pain. If your dog shows sudden signs of joint pain, take it to the veterinarian immediately. Let the veterinarian decide if the symptoms indicate Lyme disease. Also, if you find a deer tick attached to your dog, take the dog to the veterinarian after you have removed the tick. Be careful not to crush the tick between your fingers.

There is only one vaccination for Lyme disease available at the moment and it only has conditional approval. It also complicates the diagnostic problem since vaccinated dogs will test positive for the disease. As with most canine diseases, the best cure for Lyme disease is to avoid it. By using a good dip, one especially designed for ticks, using a good insect repellent, and avoiding known sites of infestation, you increase the chances of your dog not becoming infected with Lyme disease.

Leptospirosis

Like most infectious canine diseases, leptospirosis is typified by fever, loss of appetite, depression, and listlessness. Dogs infected with leptospirosis frequently show a characteristic "hunch-backed" look due to kidney infection and pain. Sometimes ulcers will form on the mucous membrane of the mouth and throat. The dog may have extreme thirst, a thick brown coat on its tongue, and increased urination as a result of the kidney infection. Blood may also be present in the stool or from the mouth. It is not uncommon for the whites of the eyes to turn yellow.

Diarrhea and vomiting are other common symptoms. In spite of the disgusting symptoms, "lepto" is usually relatively mild. Older dogs, sickly animals, or very young pups suffer most from the disease.

Leptospirosis is one of those diseases covered by the so-called "seven-in-one" injections given as the puppy's first shots. It is important that puppies have these injections, followed by annual boosters.

Other Health Problems

External Parasites

Fleas are probably the most common parasites found on dogs. Beyond the irritation and problems

Fleas become infected with tapeworms when they bite infected dogs. Healthy dogs swallow infected fleas and become infected themselves.

directly attributable to fleas, they are a common transport for other diseases and parasites. Tapeworms require the flea as a vector to get into the dog's system. Fleas cause itching, loss of hair, and, potentially, anemia. Most instances of canine eczema are related to flea infestations.

Fleas breed with amazing rapidity. Adult fleas lay eggs in whatever organic material is available. Damp bedding is an ideal place for incubating flea eggs. Six to twelve days after the eggs are laid, larval fleas hatch. The larvae eat organic material for a few days, then spin a cocoon. When the adult female flea emerges from the cocoon, it immediately attaches itself to the first dog, or other host, that comes along. After filling itself on blood, it begins laying eggs and the cycle starts all over. Since the female flea lays hundreds or thousands of eggs at time, it is easy to see how these pests can overrun a kennel.

If a flea is found on a dog it is a sure bet that the dog's environment is infested. Simply treating the dog will only give temporary benefits. If there are fleas in the house, kennel, or yard, the dog will be reinfected when it is returned to the infested area. The best treatment for fleas involves dipping the dog, cleaning and treating its kennel, and treating other areas it frequents. Fortunately, the better organophosphate-based dips and poisons have proven highly effective in killing and controlling fleas.

Recently, a systemic approach to flea control has been perfected that involves giving measured doses of a chemical monthly. The chemical prevents flea eggs from hatching and, in this way, the flea's reproductive cycle is broken. While this approach has several things in its favor, there are also a few drawbacks. Apparently, the logic behind the pill is based on the assumption that the dog being treated is the only dog around. Another problem is that this form of treatment requires that the flea bites the dog before it can take effect. In a heavily infested area the dog will still be bitten as much as it ever was. If the treated dog is allergic, it will still show classic symptoms such as loss of hair and skin irritation. While the product has not been on the market long enough to make any firm statement as to its impact, it is a good bet that traditional treatments will also have to be used in an effective treatment program.

Ticks are typically found in dense brush and woods where there is a high mammal host population. As dogs brush up against bushes containing ticks, the tick attaches itself to the dog and quickly begins to suck blood. As discussed earlier, tick bites can cause skin irritation and spread potentially fatal diseases such as Lyme disease. Deer ticks are small (1 mm to 3 mm) and hard-shelled.

They are the ticks that carry Lyme disease. The more common dog tick is larger and softer shelled.

The best way to prevent ticks is to keep your border collie away from areas known to be infested, but this approach is not realistic for most owners. The best approach for controlling ticks on your border collie is a combination of living area treatment, regular dipping, and the application of insect repellents. Some of the same dips that have proven effective against fleas also work well against ticks. Some manufacturers sell dips that are advertised as being especially effective against ticks. Talk to your veterinarian about the most effective treatment regimen for your dog and the area.

Border collies should be examined as often as possible for the presence of ticks. The dense undercoat of the breed makes it difficult to locate ticks. Smooth-haired border collies have the same undercoat and should receive the same close examination. Run your fingers through the hair on its back and sides, examine the area around and in the ears closely, checking the inside of the ears and the area just above the eyes especially closely. Have the animal lie down so that you can check the stomach, the base of the tail, and lower portions of the chest.

If you find ticks on your border collie, do not just pull them off. Simply pulling the tick off will very likely leave the parasite's head in your dog's skin, which almost always results in the area around the bite becoming infected. A better method of removing the parasites is to soak a cotton swab in alcohol and daub the area right on top of the bite. Next, using a pair of tweezers, grasp the tick as close to the skin as you can. (Never use unprotected fingers when trying to remove ticks as Lyme disease and other diseases can be transmitted to humans through contact with the skin.) Pull the tick out of the dog's skin very slowly. Make sure that none of the tick is left attached to your dog. Apply more disinfectant to the area. Find something to do with the tick—flush it down the toilet, burn it, or crush it. Just make sure that it doesn't come in contact again with you or your border collie. If you find a large tick with one or more smaller ticks around it, you have found an adult female with male suitors. The little males have to be removed in the same manner as the larger females, and as carefully.

Other owners and handlers may suggest that ticks are easily removed by applying a lighted cigarette or hot match to the tick's backside; however, there are some drawbacks to this method: It might be difficult to get a nervous border collie to sit still while you poke a hot cigarette or match at it. If you try this method and wind up burning the dog, it may be difficult to persuade it to let you try the same method again. The most convincing argument against this method is that *it just does not work.* Use the alcohol method recommended above and save yourself and your dog some pain.

Ear mites: Ear mites are another type of blood-sucking parasite that are obviously, from the name, found in the ears and ear canals. Dogs with ear mites will show excessive scratching of the ears and constant head shaking. Ear mites produce a dirty, waxy/greasy substance that adheres to the inside of the ear. While an ear mite infection is not life-threatening, it can cause your dog a great deal of discomfort and stress.

Examine your dog's ears frequently. If it shows any of the symptoms mentioned above, or has a waxy deposit in its ears, get it to a professional. Ear mites are transmitted through contact with other infected dogs. Regular examinations and professional care

are especially important if you have more than one dog.

Mange: Mange is an inflammation of the skin caused by parasitic mites. The male mites remain on the surface while the females burrow up to an inch into the skin. After laying 20 to 40 eggs, the female dies. The newly hatched mites mature in about two weeks. During this time they live on blood and lymph. As a by-product of the mite's metabolism it secretes a toxin that causes itching. Two types of mites produce two types of mange:

1. *Demodectic mange* is most common in younger dogs. This type of mange, often called red mange, is characterized by patchy hair loss.

2. *Sarcoptic mange* is sometimes called scabies. It causes the loss of large amounts of hair and intense itching and is particularly dangerous since it can pass from dog to human.

If your border collie show symptoms of mange, take it to a veterinarian as quickly as possible. Beyond the obvious problems of discomfort and unsightly skin lesions, secondary infections can cause the infected dog to die.

Internal Parasites

One of the most important parts of a complete health management program for your border collie is the control of worms. Regular testing of feces and blood by the veterinarian can detect internal parasites before they become a major problem. Treatment is best left to professionals. Veterinarians have access to a broader range of treatments than even experienced amateurs and are better versed in their use.

Dogs are most commonly affected by roundworms, hookworms, tapeworms, and heartworms. If you think your dog has internal parasites of any kind, get it to the veterinarian.

Heartworms: Forty or fifty years ago heartworms were considered a problem only in Florida and the Gulf

Coast area of the United States. Dogs in the Midwest, the Northeast, and desert areas of the United States almost never contracted heartworms; therefore, few veterinarians in those areas knew how to diagnose or treat the problem. Now, as a result of the increased mobility of the American public since the late 1960s, heartworms are found in most parts of the country.

Heartworms are transmitted from infected dogs to uninfected dogs through a mosquito bite. In fact, the heartworm requires the mosquito as a host during part of its development. There are five stages, labeled L1 through L5, in the development of a heartworm. The young heartworms of the L1 stage are better known as microfilaria. It is in the L1 stage that microfilaria are sucked into the host mosquito when the dog is bitten. While in the mosquito, the microfilaria will progress through the L2 to the L3 stage. L3 stage heartworms move to the mosquito's mouth parts and wait until the mosquito bites a dog. The heartworm larvae are deposited on the dog's skin and crawl into the bite wound left by the mosquito. These larvae live in the dog's skin until they develop into L5 larvae, at which point they enter the infected animal's bloodstream, travel to the pulmonary arteries, and develop into adult heartworms. There they start the cycle again.

Today there is no real reason for dogs to develop clinical symptoms of heartworm infestations. Preventive treatment is available in daily and monthly dosages. Daily doses are easier to remember but forgetting a single day's dose can result in a heartworm infection. Monthly doses provide longer coverage, but may be harder to remember. Talk to your veterinarian about the best plan for your dog. Do not forget to fill him or her in on your work schedule, your social life, and your memory. Remember, though, that all such treatments do is kill microfilaria; adult heartworms are left alive but sterile.

If your border collie is unfortunate enough to develop clinical symptoms of a heartworm infestation, they will develop gradually. As the number of adult heartworms increases in the pulmonary arteries, blood flow is dramatically reduced. Infected dogs will lose stamina, wheeze, cough, gag, and retch. They become listless and depressed. If the infestation is not treated, a slow death is certain. Blood flow in some dogs is reduced to the point that normally pink parts, such as the tongue, may turn blue.

Heartworm treatment has improved greatly in recent years. Older heartworm treatments used highly toxic products that were as likely to kill the dog as they were the heartworms. Modern treatment is still a long, dangerous process but it is better managed and safer than it has ever been. Seeing a dog infected with heartworms or one that has had heartworm treatments is the best incentive for keeping your pet on a regular preventive program. It should be noted that heartworm treatments may also prevent hookworms and roundworms.

Roundworms: If you notice that your border collie's coat has lost its shine, or that younger dogs have developed a massive belly, the dog may have roundworms. They are more common in puppies and young dogs. Roundworms are rarely fatal, but they reduce an animal's vitality and potential. Severe roundworm infestations, left untreated, may result in a stunted adult.

Dogs with roundworms will frequently vomit worms or pass them in their stools. At the first sign of roundworms, get your border collie to the veterinarian as soon as possible. Better yet, prevent roundworm infes-

Heartworm larvae are spread from infected dogs to healthy ones. The larvae can develop into adults in the dog's heart, resulting in damage or death.

tations in your border collie by keeping its kennel or living area clean. Dogs get roundworms through contact with roundworm-infected feces. By keeping your dog's living area stool-free, you decrease your dog's chances of infection. Regular visits to the veterinarian for testing and treatment are also key to reducing damage by these parasites. Remember that dog food costs money, and every roundworm present in your dog takes some of what you are feeding the dog. Instead of a healthy border collie you may be raising a brood of extremely healthy roundworms.

Hookworms: Hookworms get their name from the hooks they use to attach themselves to the host animal's stomach. Once attached, they go on to suck blood from the linings of the stomach and intestines.

Hookworms are especially harmful to puppies, but can attack dogs of any age. Infected dogs may have bloody or tarry stools and become "unthrifty." They may lose their appetite, lose weight, or fail to gain weight. Some dogs may die due to anemia or complications from anemia.

This is another case where clean kennels can reduce the chance of infestation. Combine cleanliness with regular checkups and treatment. An aggressive treatment program combined with rigorous kennel cleanliness should reduce the effects of hookworms.

Tapeworms: The tapeworm cycle begins with an infected host. Tapeworms deposit eggs in fecal matter. Some of this fecal matter clings to hair around the anus. Fleas inadvertently swallow the eggs. The tapeworm eggs undergo some development inside the flea and when the flea later bites the dog, the dog naturally chews at the bite. If it swallows an infected flea while it is gnawing, the dog is infected and an adult tapeworm will develop.

The first part of the tapeworm to develop is the head, or scolex. The scolex has several hooks around the top, which are used to attach the scolex to the lining of the stomach. Once attached, the tapeworm absorbs nutrients from the dog's stomach and shortly begins to produce body segments known as proglottids. The youngest, smallest proglottid is attached to the head. Larger, more mature proglottids are at the other end of the tapeworm. Tapeworms may have several thousand proglottids, each bigger and more mature than the one before it. Proglottids contain both ovaries and testes. By the time mature proglottids separate from the tapeworm, they will contain a number of fertilized eggs. Dog owners may notice what appears to be rice around the dog's anus. These "rice kernels" are the adult proglottids that have passed through the dog.

Your border collie does not have to be heavily infested with fleas to contract tapeworms; it only takes one flea to convey the worms. Fortunately, tapeworms are rarely fatal. Like roundworms they will absorb as much food as they can from your dog's stomach. Puppies cannot achieve their full potential if they have heavy tapeworm infestations. If you see evidence of tapeworms on your dog, consult your veterinarian for treatment.

Emergencies

Poisons

Keeping a border collie away from poisons can be particularly difficult as most of the poisons that it may encounter are not labeled. Even chocolate can kill a dog; a fatal dose can be surprisingly small.

As discussed in Puppy-Proofing Your Home, beginning on page 40, there are many dangerous substances to watch out for in and around your home, such as:
• Most paint-related products such as paint removers, varnishes, turpentine, and oil-based paints.
• Kerosene, gasoline, diesel fuel, and cleaning fluid.
• Rat poisons, hand soaps, detergents, insecticides, mothballs, polishes, and some beauty products.
• Antifreeze. Unless prevented from doing so, dogs will drink antifreeze when they will not drink water. It is widely held that antifreeze tastes sweet to dogs, although there is no way of determining exactly what the dogs find attractive about antifreeze.
• Various plants (see chart on page 41). Jimpson weed, mistletoe, foxglove, and poinsettia leaves are as poisonous to dogs as they are to humans. Leaves of common ivy are also poisonous as are daffodils, tulip bulbs, lily of the valley, azaleas, wisteria, and delphiniums. Before you decorate or buy a potted plant, talk to your veterinarian and a good horticulturist concerning a plant's harmful potential.

• Contact with toads can cause your border collie to foam at the mouth and/or die.

• Some species of shrews are also poisonous.

• Spiders, scorpions, some flies, and butterflies, even cockroaches, may be fatally poisonous if eaten in enough quantity.

If you have reason to believe that your dog has ingested a petroleum-based poison, an acid, or a strongly alkaline substance, *do not induce vomiting*. Call your veterinarian. If your dog can drink, give it as much milk as it will take. Have someone read the label on the container the poison came in to see if an antidote is identified. If the poison has an antidote and it is available, administer it. After you have exercised all these options, get your dog to the veterinarian as quickly as possible.

If the poison is of another type, induce vomiting by giving the dog a mixture of equal parts water and hydrogen peroxide. Try to give at least one tablespoon of the mixture per 10 pounds (4.5 kg) of body weight. Make a pocket of the dog's lips and pour a little of the mixture into the pocket at a time. Allow the dog time enough to swallow the liquid before giving it more. Vomiting should begin a few minutes after the final dose is administered. After vomiting ends, give the animal a teaspoon of Epsom salts mixed with water to empty the intestines. When your pet is purged, take it to the veterinary emergency room as quickly as possible.

Heatstroke

Border collies have been successfully worked in the most extreme environments; they work reindeer in Greenland and sheep in the deserts of Arizona. They are, however, susceptible to heatstroke. When you design and build your kennels, make sure that the dogs have sufficient shade in the warmer parts of the year. Also, be sure not to close up your dog in a car or truck at any time. Even in temperatures that may not seem warm to a human, the temperature in a vehicle can rise to dangerous levels. The bed of your pickup truck can also produce extremely high temperatures. If you make a habit of riding around in a truck with your border collie, remember that the practice is unsafe in a number of ways.

Another thing to remember about border collies is that they do not have an "off" switch. If they become involved in something they enjoy doing, it is difficult to tell when they have become overheated. Quite a few ranchers and farmers have lost good dogs because they worked them up to the point where they died. Keep a close watch on your dog. If it becomes dazed, runs a high fever, or shows extremely red gums and lips, get it to water. If you happen to be close to a garden hose, use it to soak the dog. If you are near a pond, pool, or water trough, put the dog in. If you are close enough to your emergency kit, soak the overheated border collie with alcohol and water. Then get it to the veterinarian.

If your puppy suffers the symptoms of heatstroke, cool him by covering him with a wet towel. Do not use ice or ice water, because it could cause shock.

HOW-TO:
Treating Automobile Accident Victims

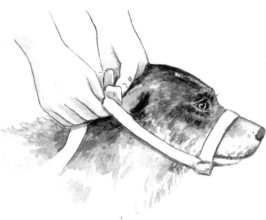

In an emergency, a muzzle can be made of a leash, a belt, or a pair of pantyhose.

Aside from poisons and diseases, the border collie's only natural enemy is the automobile. No matter how hard you may have tried to protect your dog from accidents, they may still happen. If your dog is struck by an automobile, take the following steps:

1. Stay calm. Speak softly. Do not panic. If you go berserk, you can expect no more of your dog.

2. Loosen the dog's collar. Check its breathing passages for secretions or other blockages. If they exist, clear the passageways.

3. Protect yourself. Do not poke or prod at an injured dog. No matter how trustworthy your border collie has been in the past, all bets are off once it is injured. Many owners have been unpleasantly surprised when their pet mauled them as they were trying to relieve its discomfort. Before you try to examine your pet, make sure there is a muzzle in place unless the injured dog is having difficulty breathing. If a commercially made muzzle is not available, make a temporary muzzle out of whatever you can find— leashes, belts, stockings, or neckties. Make a loop out of the object, cross the loose ends under the dog's muzzle and around its neck, and tie the ends securely behind the head. Test the muzzle to make sure the injured animal cannot bite.

4. Attend to any bleeding that you find. Clean the wound and apply pressure until the bleeding stops. Heavy bleeding may require that you apply more than one bandage. Keep applying bandages until the bleeding stops. If the bleeding cannot be stopped with pressure, apply a tourniquet. Place the tourniquet between the heart and the wound and gradually increase the pressure until the bleeding stops. Once the bleeding has stopped, release the tourniquet every fifteen minutes to keep the wound clean.

5. If there is a sucking chest wound involved, it must be plugged. The wound allows air to be drawn into the chest cavity rather than the lungs. Use a piece of plastic wrap or some other nonporous material to cover the wound, and some adhesive tape to secure the edges. The idea is to prevent air from entering the wound so that your dog will be able to breathe as normally as possible.

6. Stomach wounds offer other problems. Cover exposed

If bleeding cannot be stopped by the application of pressure, apply a tourniquet between the wound and the dog's heart.

intestines with a wet, sterile dressing. It is important to keep the intestines and organs from drying, to keep infection to a minimum, and to keep the intestines in the body cavity. Wrap the sterile dressing with a commercial bandage if it is available.

Do not attempt to push protruding intestines back into the stomach cavity. Pressure on the intestines may cause weak spots in the intestines to leak their contents into the body cavity, which can result in peritonitis, an infection of the lining of the stomach cavity. At best, peritonitis can be troublesome to the dog's recovery. At worst, it can be fatal.

7. For head wounds, pressure should be applied using a gauze pad to reduce bleeding. Hold the pad in place with tape. Remember that even minor head wounds can bleed profusely. Make sure your pet is conscious and that it stays that way.

8. Puncture wounds should be allowed to bleed for a few minutes as the bleeding will help clean the wound. If bleeding is

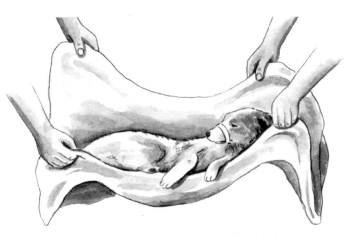

An injured dog may be moved on a board, a towel, or blanket.

very heavy, apply pressure with a gauze pad. Hold the pad in place until the bleeding stops.

9. Check for signs of shock— weakness, pale gums, shivering, or a faint pulse. Keep the dog warm. Treat any bleeding wound it might have and try to keep it conscious.

10. Do not move the injured dog unless you must. Some veterinarians will come to accident sites, but if you must move your dog to go to the veterinarian, try

to find help. Try to gently move the animal with a piece of plywood, a tarp, or even a large serving tray. If you have to move the animal by yourself, try easing your pet onto a blanket. Then gently drag the injured animal to a vehicle and try to get it into it without causing further harm.

11. Call ahead to make sure that someone will be waiting for you at the veterinary clinics.

12. Hurry.

Administering Medicine

When administering liquid medicine, pull the dog's lips into a pocket and pour the medicine into the lip pocket, holding the dog's mouth closed until it has swallowed all the medicine. Tilting the animal's head back too far or pouring the liquid medicine directly over its tongue can result in inhalation pneumonia, and pneumonia of any kind can result in death.

Pills are best administered by pressing your dog's lips firmly against its teeth, forcing its mouth open. Place the pill as far back on the dog's tongue as possible. Close the animal's mouth and hold it shut until you are certain that the pill has been swallowed. Stick around for a few minutes to make sure that the dog does not spit the pill out on the floor.

When administering medicine at home, follow the veterinarian's schedule and dosage instructions. *Never* give your dog human drugs unless instructed to do so by your veterinarian.

Administer liquid medicine by forming a pocket in the cheeks, tilting the head back slightly and pouring the medicine into the pocket. Hold the dog's mouth closed until it swallows.

Life Expectancy

Border collies are midsized dogs, and, as such, they tend to live longer than larger breeds. It is not uncommon to find 12-year-old border collies still working around the ranch. Admittedly, 12-year-old dogs work slower than younger dogs, but they can work. Even 17-year-old border collies are not unheard of. When choosing a border collie, do not worry about life expectancy. Pick a bright, healthy puppy from a good line. If given proper nutrition, veterinary care, and attention, it is likely to be around for a while.

Old Age and Your Border Collie

Border collies age gracefully; however, they do mature less rapidly than many other dog breeds. Some British handlers do not consider a dog mature until "it has a year under each paw," or until the dog is four years old. Most border collies cannot be considered full-grown until they are least 18 months old. Slow maturation is coupled with longevity in this case. As mentioned above, 12-year-old border collies are not uncommon.

There comes a time, however, when the border collie slows down. This will vary from dog to dog due to bloodlines, health, early nutrition, and the cumulative effects of any injuries it may have received. Even with a near-perfect set of circumstances, dogs gray and become less active. Even when the dog becomes incapable of keeping up with its normal activities, it will make every effort to do so. Its dietary needs will change. Special areas of focus concerning its health will change and require more care. Care of the teeth, ears, eyes, and feet will become more important as your border collie ages. Talk to your veterinarian about your dog's specific needs.

Not every border collie will have the intensity of this handsome creature, but intensity is characteristic of the breed.

Euthanasia

If you are very lucky your border collie will live a long, healthy life and die quietly in its sleep. Unfortunately, older border collies sometimes develop chronic painful conditions, and younger dogs may be afflicted with cancers or orthopedic problems that can not only cripple them but keep them in pain. It is at this point that you, as the owner, will have to decide whether or not to have your friend euthanized. The decision, as difficult as it may be, should be based on logic. You should ask yourself if your dog is suffering and if that suffering will end in the near future. If the animal is in pain, can the pain be controlled with chemicals? Can surgery repair the dog's problems? Will your dog have any quality of life after treatment?

If the answer to these questions is "No," the decision may have to be made to euthanize your companion. Euthanasia can offer a sick and suffering animal an easing of pain and a quick release from depression. Talk to your veterinarian about your options and your border collie's condition. There are times when the hardest decision you will ever have to make is also the most humane.

Breeding

Should You Breed Your Border Collie?

There is always a temptation as a beloved pet ages to want to preserve it, at least genetically. Life without Moss or Fleet or Hope or Craig may be daunting and unimaginable to the fond owner. If you own a border collie and find yourself in this situation, you may decide to breed Mist just so you can have part of her around. Old Tweed may have been a big help around the farm and the possibility of a pup from him, with the same working characteristics, is a pleasant thought. Before you embark on a breeding project, however, there are some things you should ask yourself:

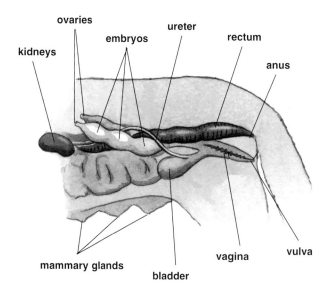

Female reproductive glands.

kidneys

ovaries

embryos

ureter

rectum

anus

mammary glands

bladder

vagina

vulva

1. Is your border collie truly exceptional? Has it done anything to make it stand out from other border collies? Is it an exceptional cowdog or sheepdog? How far did it go in obedience training? Was it outstanding in any other way? If your border collie has not excelled at anything except being lovable, consider buying a pup from somewhere else.
2. Is your border collie genetically perfect? Have its hips, joints, and eyes been examined and certified? Does your pet have allergies? Has it developed an autoimmune problem such as lupus? Your veterinarian should be able to provide you with most of this information, if he or she has not already. If your border collie is not genetically perfect, do not breed it under any circumstances.
3. If the border collie you intend to breed is a bitch that you own, do you have the facilities to whelp and raise a litter of pups? Remember that a litter is likely to be more puppies than the one or two you intend to keep. Can you provide a warm, dry, safe place for the puppies and the bitch? Keeping a border collie or two in the house is considerably different from having a litter of eight or nine six-week-old puppies gallivanting around the place.
4. Are you willing and able to make the financial investment for the veterinary and dietary costs that pregnancy, whelping, and early puppyhood will entail? To get a good estimate, talk to your veterinarian or another breeder about per-puppy costs.
5. What is the market for border collie puppies in your area? Is the market already flooded? Is there much of a

demand for the breed at all? Unless you are willing to keep six or eight more border collies than you need, you must have some place to send them.

6. Are the same bloodlines still available? Are younger brothers or sisters of your border collie around? Does the breeder where you got your pet have nieces or nephews of the dog you plan to breed? Since almost all the characteristics we have come to associate with border collies are polygenic, the probability that you are going to produce a clone of your border collie are extremely low. If any puppies are available, consider purchasing one rather than going to all the time and expense of breeding.

Questions #1 and #2 are absolutes; border collies that do not get a "Yes" to both questions should not be considered for breeding. A negative response to #3 should also discourage you, unless you start planning far enough in advance. Veterinary costs for the puppies and the bitch can be daunting. If the answer to question #5 is "Not much" or "I don't know," you might put more emphasis on question #4. Question #6 may offer the best of all possible worlds: a puppy of similar bloodlines to your own without the effort and expense of breeding.

In summary, there are more good reasons for not breeding your border collie than for breeding it.

Working or Show Qualities for Breeding

If your border collie passes muster, you will have to make more decisions. The first decision you have to make is what characteristics you want in your border collie. The answer to this question should be determined by what you want from the puppies.

Working Stock

If you have working border collie stock and want working puppies, you

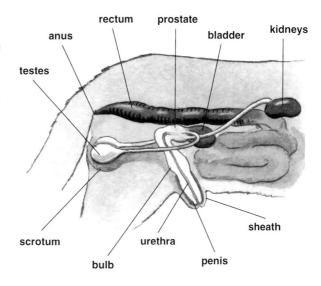

Male reproductive glands.

have only one choice. You must decide what characteristics you want in a border collie, track down your ideal border collie of the sex opposite yours, and breed to it. Looking for the ideal working border collie may involve going from breeder to breeder and trial to trial. Time invested in selecting the best working border collie you can find for breeding to your dog is time well spent.

Obedience Dogs

If you want to use your puppies in obedience, your choices are more complex. Although there are a lot of excellent obedience dogs available, not many obedience trainers breed their own puppies. You may be able to find an outstanding obedience border collie to breed to yours, but you also have the same option as most obedience trainers: You can breed your border collie to the best working stock you can find. The working border collie will bring

The two younger puppies may well be younger siblings of the older red border collie.

bloodlines that will provide intelligence, athleticism, and ready acceptance of training, characteristics that are all you really need for obedience work.

Show Dogs

If you plan to breed with an eye for the bench, you will have more decisions and more problems. For starters, there is not a large pool of bench border collies around. Conformation shows for border collies are a relatively recent development so availability of such stock will be limited. You should also consider exactly what you want to do with the puppies. Do you want to work the puppies, compete in obedience or agility trials, or compete in flyball or Frisbee competitions? Do you just want an intelligent pet? Once you have answered these questions, you can select the significant other in your border collie's life.

The Canine Estrous Cycle

Most border collie bitches will not come into heat until they are about one year old, but there is a great deal of variation in when a female will begin to cycle. Some will go into heat at seven months of age while others may not begin to cycle until they are eighteen months old, but, in general, if the bitch remains healthy and well fed, she will go into heat every six months. It is important when breeding your bitch that you wait until she is mature enough; just because she has come into heat does not mean that she is ready to breed. Two years or older is generally old enough but consult with your veterinarian to be sure.

The canine estrous cycle is potentially made up of four stages: *proestrus, estrus, metestrus*, and *anestrus*.

Proestrus

The beginning of the canine estrous cycle is typified by vaginal swelling and a blood-tinged discharge from the vagina. At the same time the external signs of proestrus are occurring, changes are going on internally: In the ovaries, ova begin to develop and mature, and the uterus wall begins to swell in preparation for the implantation of the fertilized eggs.

On average, proestrus will last nine days, but some bitches will have a proestrus period of four to five days, while others may have a proestrus period as long as fourteen days. During proestrus, male dogs will begin to show interest in the bitch. She will not be terribly appreciative of those attentions, and, at this point, a lot of posturing and snapping will occur if a male is allowed near her.

At the first sign of proestrus, the bitch should be confined in a male-proof pen or kennel. She should not be confined with any male other than the chosen sire. Even male puppies as young as six months should be kept away from a bitch in heat.

Estrus

During estrus, the blood-tinged discharge thickens and becomes clearer.

Ovulation occurs during this phase of estrous and the female will become fertile and receptive to the advances of male dogs. During this phase, the selected sire is introduced to the female. Estrus may last as long as nine days but is typically much shorter.

During this phase, no male except the selected sire should be allowed contact with the female.

Metestrus

Metestrus occurs if the female is impregnated. Her body changes to get ready for the development and birth of puppies. The teats will begin to swell in preparation for milk production.

Anestrus

If the bitch passes through estrus without breeding or conceiving, she will enter anestrus. Anestrus is the latency phase that nonpregnant, non-nursing bitches are in most of the time. During anestrus, vaginal discharge will cease, the vagina will return to normal size, and the ovaries and uterus shrink to pre-proestrus size and appearance. All reproductive organs will enter an inactive period, waiting to become active again in six months or so.

Mating

There is a part of copulation in domestic dogs that frequently surprises—and shocks—some first-time breeders—the tie. After "normal" copulation occurs, the male will appear to be "stuck" in the female's vagina. The reason that he appears to be stuck is because he is, but, after a few minutes, the happy couple will wind up standing haunch to haunch. There will very likely be a few awkward moments from the dismount to the haunch-to-haunch position. None of this calls for any human intervention. The whole process is normal; in fact, the whole process is necessary. The male's penis swells, which causes the pair to

be tied. During the tie, sperm is not lost and other males cannot breed the female. Eventually, they will come apart, but give them 15 minutes to an hour of semiprivacy.

The mating pair will breed repeatedly if left together. Some breeders will remove the male from the female's pen, or vice versa. A day or two later the male may be reintroduced, and, if the female is still in estrus, she will breed again.

At no time during estrus should any other male be allowed around the female. It is a common misconception that once a female is bred, she will not conceive from another male. There are two flaws in this logic: The first male may not have impregnated the female—any male that copulates with the female afterward may sire her puppies. The second problem is that it is entirely possible for a bitch to have puppies by more than one sire at the same whelping. Theoretically, it is possible for each puppy in an eight-puppy litter to have a different sire. Statistically, it is about as probable as being hit by a falling meteorite, but it is possible. It is not at all uncommon for two sires to be represented in a single litter.

Wiping on orphan neonate's belly to stimulate defecation and urination.

Pregnancy

If everything worked as planned, you should have a pregnant border collie bitch. For the next two months or so, she will look increasingly pregnant. While 63 days is typically given as the length of gestation, a normal pregnancy may vary in length from 58 to 63 days with no ill effects on mother or pups.

During pregnancy, the bitch's teats will swell and turn a brighter pink, depending on her coloration. Her stomach will swell as the puppies in her uterus grow. It is normal for a border collie bitch to put on a good deal of weight during pregnancy, but it is critical that the weight she gains be mostly puppy. Excessive fat in a bitch can lead to complications at birth, early delivery, and general poor-health. Some breeders will try to provide the bitch's much increased protein requirement by feeding a high-quality puppy chow for the last third of the pregnancy.

Keep your pregnant border collie active and in shape. Unless you work your border collie bitch on rank stock, you will need to phase out her work schedule slowly. Three weeks before the due date, all females should be allowed to retire from their jobs. If you use your border collie bitch on dangerous stock, she should be retired from such work when she is found to be pregnant. One good kick by an ill-tempered cow or a strong butt from a protective ewe could end your hope for puppies in short order.

Whelping

If you work a full-time job, you will have to make arrangements to be available to help your border collie whelp. Whelping will normally take place 56 to 63 days into the pregnancy. It is not likely that you will actually have to assist in the delivery, as border collies have comparatively few problems delivering puppies. It is recommended that you be present at the delivery, however, in case things do not go as smoothly as they should.

You will need to find some place for the bitch to whelp. The best place for the blessed event to occur is in your home. Find an area in your home that is relatively private. Other indoor dogs and children should be kept away from the new mother. Border collie bitches are no more protective of their puppies than any other breed, but, if their puppies are bothered by another pet or a child, they may react violently. Such violence is typically more bluff than actual biting, but other pets, children, or the puppies may get hurt in the disturbance.

The Whelping Box

You will also need a specially designed box for your border collie to whelp in. The whelping box should be square, about 24 inches (61 cm) longer than your bitch measures from nose tip to the base of her tail. The bottom should be solid half-inch plywood. The sides should be 12 inches

The whelping box is designed with a ledge that provides the puppies with a safe place to escape mother.

94

(30 cm) in height. A 12-inch ledge should be built on the inside of the box to allow the puppies a safe place to get away from Mom and still be near her. The sides and the ledges should be easily removable from the floor.

Pig railing is also an option—vertical bars from the floor to the ledge that let puppies through without allowing Mom to get a leg into the sleeping litter. Rails should be roughly 6 inches (15 cm) apart to provide access to the puppies while being small enough to keep Mom at bay.

Line the box with common black-and-white newspaper, no color print, as color inks can be toxic to varying degrees. Make sure there are several layers of newsprint in your whelping box. Removing a layer of newsprint is less disturbing to the pups and the new mother than pulling it all up and replacing it. It also leaves a familiar smell for the bitch and the pups.

There should also be an outside source of heat. An overhead source of infrared light will serve well but remember that the extra heat is only for litters born in colder weather. No matter how concerned you are for mother and pups, you do not need to overheat them. Unless the puppies show signs of being cold, let the mother provide their heat. Newborn border collie puppies will be comfortable at 85°F (29°C). If the ambient temperature drops much below 85°F, provide a safe form of external warmth such as a light or a specially designed heating pad. Keep the dial on its lowest setting and wrap the pad tightly in an old towel. Always make sure the puppies have enough room next to the pad to escape the heat.

Puppy Care

Puppy care should begin at the moment of birth. If at all possible, you should be present during whelping and, if you have a friend who has more experience than you in assisting a whelping bitch, it is perfectly all right to have that friend present as well. What you will want to avoid is the circuslike atmosphere that some first-time breeders create. There is very little need for anyone but the breeder and an experienced helper to be around. Too many people around the whelping box can make a bitch nervous and cause problems with the delivery. However, do have an emergency number handy for your border collie's veterinarian. If serious complications occur, that is the kind of support you will need.

Temperature: If the air temperature where you have decided you want the birth to take place is below 85 to 90°F (29–32°C), keep an eye on the puppies as they are born. Let the mother do as much as she can in cleaning and encouraging the puppies. Once she turns back to deliver the next pup, dry the last one born and make sure that it is warm enough. You may have to wrap the puppies in a soft cloth until they dry enough to not be bothered by drafts and temperature changes. While you are drying the newborn, tie off its umbilical cord close to its body with dental floss. Use scissors to trim off excess cord. Be sure that the puppies remain as close to their mother as possible. Be certain that every puppy has located a teat and is nursing.

A border collie mother nursing a litter will require increased amounts of food in order to keep her and her pups in top condition.

This chubby merled border collie puppy has shown its true colors early in life.

Veterinary care: Sickly puppies should be taken to a veterinarian. Better yet, have the veterinarian come to your house as soon after the birth as possible. New puppies must not be exposed to outside sources of infection until they have completed their inoculations. At age six weeks, puppies should get their temporary shots. These and the permanent shots required later should be administered by your veterinarian.

Elimination: Once your pups have eaten, wait for them to eliminate. If you are in a hurry or the pups are slow to perform, use a wet washcloth to stimulate them. Clean up the mess by peeling off a layer or two of newspapers. Remove the newspapers from the room, or kennel, with the puppies and secure it for disposal. All droppings and urine-stained newspaper should be removed from the whelping/holding box as soon as possible. Instant cleanness will keep odor and flies to a minimum.

Dewclaws: After the puppies are warm and nursing, you will have to ask yourself whether you want to remove their dewclaws, those claws located in the inside of the leg, slightly higher than the footpads. In some breeds of dog, the dewclaw is always removed. Other breeds, such as the Pyrenees, retain the dewclaws as one of the defining traits of the breed. In border collies it really does not matter. Dogs imported from Britain almost uniformly have their dewclaws removed, as British handlers and trainers fear the accidental loss of the dewclaw in the heather. The United States has precious little heather, but does have a lot of rough terrain. If you feel that a dewclaw would be detrimental to your pup's performance or health, have your veterinarian remove them before the puppies turn three days old.

Surrogate Mother

If something unusual happens to the bitch, you may find yourself being a surrogate mother for a litter of puppies. A small percentage of border collie bitches die whelping; others develop mastitis and are unable to nurse their pups; still others may be killed by accidents. In any event, it is you who will have to feed the puppies, clean up after them, and make sure that they are clean.

If you do lose the services of the mother, obtain several bottles and some canine milk replacer from your veterinarian. Then try to arrange your puppies' schedule so that you can get some sleep. Newborn border collie puppies are voracious eaters. They will eat until they can't eat any more, eliminate, sleep, and want to eat again. Figure on feeding your pups every four hours. You can be sure that they will be ready for you at that time. Carefully record the amount each puppy eats. Puppies should be weighed at the same time every day and records kept of weight gain and/or loss.

If it becomes necessary to assist delivery, grasp the pup's shoulders and apply gentle traction downward.

Weaning

No matter who feeds your puppies, you should start the transition to solid food around three weeks of age. Start with a premium-quality puppy chow. Mix some warm milk or milk replacer with a small amount of puppy food. Let the milk/food mix sit long enough for the feed to become soft. Put the mush in a broad, flat-bottomed stainless steel pan that should be large enough to get all members of the litter around it, at least at first. It should also be low enough that the rampaging members of the litter will have a difficult time capsizing the pan. Being stainless steel, it will be much easier to clean after every feeding.

One method of getting three-week-old puppies to eat the new mix is to let them walk through the mix and lick it

These healthy border collie puppies will require care, training, and dedication from their owners to achieve their full potential.

As part of their socialization, border collies should be introduced to a wide variety of people.

off their feet. Some puppies in the same litter will stop in the middle of the pan and begin eating the first time they are exposed to it, while others will stop at the edge, sniff, and then eat. At any rate, your puppies will be eating in short order. Over the next two to three weeks, gradually increase the amount of food in the mix. At age six weeks, they should be eating mostly puppy food. Water should be kept nearby but not in the whelping box. Use a stainless steel pan similar to the one you use for the mother's water.

Another method to get your litter to accept a commercial puppy food is to stick your hand in the food and let the members of the litter lick it. It will not take them long to go from your fingers to the contents of a nearby pan.

Note: When a pup begins to eat solid food, its mother will cease to clean up after it, therefore, feed the pups outside the whelping box in an easily cleaned area.

Gradually reduce the puppies' access to their mother, starting at about age six weeks. Over time, Mom will help you in the weaning process. Working together, you can get them all weaned at age eight to ten weeks.

Changes in the Mother's Coat

Do not be alarmed if, after weaning, your rough-haired bitch turns into a smooth-haired bitch. The rapid change in hormones that occurs in the nursing and weaning border collie bitch causes most of them to lose a large part of their hair. Some will lose hair during lactation; others will not have obvious hair loss until after weaning. Either way, it is a normal part of the whelping/nursing process. In a month or six weeks, your female will be well on the way to having her hair back.

Smooth-haired bitches will also lose some hair, but they start with hair so short that the comparison is not as dramatic. If you see hair loss occurring in your female after she whelps, do what you can to provide the nutrients she needs in her diet and do not worry.

Early Socialization

Socialization in a border collie's life should start early and continue right up to the day it dies. Socialization is a learning process that introduces the puppy to a range of people in its environment and teaches it that there is nothing to fear from humans.

There are a number of ways of breaking socialization into logical units:
1. Get started early. As soon as you have things to do around the puppies, start scratching them behind the ears and rubbing their stomachs. Let them know that you represent a pleasant experience. Make casual contact with your border collies a regular practice for as long as you have the pups.
2. Make socialization a family or community process. Get as many people involved in it as possible. If you have children of a responsible age, have

them come by when the puppies are being fed just to hold and pet them. If you have neighbors and friends who are interested in border collies, have them stop over and spend time with your pups. The more folks you have around your border collies when they are puppies, the easier their future transitions and meeting new acquaintances will be.

3. Make sure all the handling is benign. Watch children to make sure that the puppies are not picked up by their ears or hurt in any way. As the puppies get older, make sure that the wrestling and roughhousing that is normal for children and puppies does not occur. Puppies that are hurt are less likely to be trusting of anyone, and therefore less likely to be trainable.

4. Spend as much time alone with each puppy in the litter as possible.

5. Take the pups with you when go places. This is particularly true of puppies you plan to keep. Take older puppies singly to nonthreatening locations as you do chores or run errands. Remember, however, it is better to pursue this line of socialization after they have had their permanent shots.

Finally, before you decide to breed border collies, examine your own motives. You will make money from breeding border collies only if the puppies you are producing are exceptional in some way. Unproven border collie puppies, even from good stock, do not bring prices comparable to other breeds. The costs are pretty much the same.

The result of good breeding, health management, and nutrition is healthy puppies—like this gorgeous specimen.

Useful Addresses and Literature

Clubs

Border Collie Registries

The American Kennel Club (AKC)
51 Madison Avenue
New York, New York, 10010
(212) 696-8200

For Registration Information:
The American Kennel Club (AKC)
5580 Centerview Drive
Suite 200
Raleigh, North Carolina 27606

The American Border Collie
Association Inc. (ABCA)
82 Rogers Road
Perkinston, Mississippi 39573
(601) 928-7551

The American-International Border
Collie Registry, Inc. (AIBC)
1534 E. 36th Street
Des Moines, Iowa
(515) 262-8152

The North American Sheep Dog
Society (NASDS)
RR 3
McLeansboro, Illinois 62859

The Kennel Club
I-4 Clarges Street, Piccadilly
London, W1Y8AB, England

The International Sheep Dog Society
(ISDS)
Chesam House
47 Bromham Road
Bedford, England MK40 2AA

The Australian National Kennel
Council
Royal Show Grounds
Ascot Vale
Victoria, Australia

The United Kennel Club (UKC)
100 East Kilgore Road
Kalamazoo, Michigan 49001

World Wide Kennel Club
PO Box 62
Mt. Vernon, New York

Border Collie Rescue

North American Border Collie Rescue
Network, Inc. (NABCRN)
Box 843
Ithaca, New York 14851
(315) 587-3369

Border Collie Breed Clubs

The Australian Border Collie
Society
Pitt Town, NSW 2756, Australia

The Border Collie Club of Great
Britain
Firbeck, Worksop
Nottinghamshire, England

Border Collie Society of America, Inc
(BCSA)
815 Royal Oaks Drive
Durham, North Carolina 27712

The United States Border Collie
Club
Route 1, Box 83-D
Julian, Pennsylvania 16844

Books

Arthur Allen. *A Lifetime with the Working Collie, Their Training and History*. McLeansboro, IL: 1979.
—— *Border Collies in America*. McLeansboro, IL: 1965.

Caius, D. J. *Of English Dogges*. London: , 1570.

Carpenter, Barbara. *The Blue Riband of the Heather: The Supreme Champions 1906–88*. Ipswich: Farming Press, 1989.

Carpenter, E. B. *The Border Collies, Basic Training for Sheepwork*. Lydney, Glos.: M. D. Jenkins, 1982.

Drabble, Phil. *One Man and His Dog*. London: Michael Joseph, 1984.

Evans, Foy. *Border Collie Training Simplified*. City: Foy Evans, 1981.

Halsall, Eric. *British Sheepdogs*. International Sheepdog Society, 1992.

Halsall, Eric. *Sheepdogs, My Faithful Friends*. London: P. Stephens, 1980.

Karrasch, Dick. *Training A Stockdog— For Beginners*. Alabama: Karrasch, 1985.

McCaig, Donald. *Nop's Trials*. New York: Crown, 1984.

Mundell, Matt. *Country Diary*. Edinburgh: Gordon Wright Publishing, 1981.

Robertson, Pope. *Anybody Can Do It*. Elgin, TX: Rovar Publ., 1979.

Templeton, John and Matt Mundell. *Working Sheepdogs: Management and Training*. Ramsbury, Marlborough: The Crowood Press, 1988.

Varnon, Jim. *Because of Eve*. DeSoto, TX: Eve Publishing, 1986.

Periodicals

American Border Collie
12056 Mt. Vernon Avenue, #303
Grand Terrace, California 92324

Borderlines
322 Spring Branch Lane
Kennedale, Texas 76060
Fax: (817) 561-2662

The National Stock Dog Magazine
312 Portland Road
Waterloo, Wisconsin 53594

The Ranch Dog Trainer
Rt. 2, Box 333
West Plains, Missouri 65775

The Shepherd's Dogge
Woolgather Farm
Box 843
Ithaca, New York

The Working Border Collie Magazine
14933 Kirkwood Road
Sidney, Ohio 45365

United States Border Collie Club Newsletter
Route 1, Box 83-D
Julian, Pennsylvania 16844

Index